Jesus
Needs
A Body

Elizabeth R. Vaughan, M.D.

Library of Congress Cataloging-in-Publication Data

ISBN: (Print) 978-1-48359-725-6 (Ebook) 978-1-48359-726-3

Printed in the United States of America

Contents

Dedication

I would like to dedicate this book to Geri Hudson Morgan (September 25, 1939 - July 23, 2016), an extraordinary woman of God. This book is replete with references to Geri because God put us together as a ministry team, carrying the Gospel of Jesus Christ to the nations of the world for forty-two years. It was my honor and privilege to work with her and see God flow through her. It is said of Jesus, "In Him was life, and the life was the light of men" (John 1:4). Geri carried His life in her. She carried His light in her. And wherever she went, she left a trail of new friends—whether it was meeting Barbara Bush in the silk market of Beijing, China, or meeting the maid that cleaned the hotel room in San Francisco. They were all important to her, and she called them all friends. Geri liked repeating a saying she once heard. "You can tell the character of a person by the way they treat someone from whom they receive nothing." That exemplified Geri. All people, great or small, were valuable to her.

She had an uncanny knack of finding things that were blemished or broken and cleaning them up to make them shine. She would take a glass vase she bought at the thrift store for fifty cents that had a handle missing, and put it next to a vase that was perfect and expensive. She would put them both side by side in a lighted display case and think they were both equally beautiful. Of course, she would turn the part where the handle was broken off toward the wall, so its blemish would not be seen. She did that with people too, loving them for the good in them and overlooking their imperfections.

She had a huge heart, loving every facet of life. Looking around her home, you could see pictures of her journeys, her friends, dogs that she had twenty years ago, people playing golf or tennis, or boating, or horseback riding—life, life, life was everywhere, which was a reflection of who she was. She was brave enough and full of enough faith to follow me on what seemed to be impossible journeys, like building a five-million-watt television station in the Dallas/Ft. Worth Metroplex or building an eye surgery center in Beijing, China. Most people would have said that it was impossible and refused to go along with such wild ideas, but not Geri. You could count her in as long as she knew God was in it. She would never say a discouraging word. She would pack her bags, and say, "Let's go."

You have heard the saying, "God gives the best to those who leave the choice to Him." I left the choice of a ministry partner to Him, and He gave me the best—her name was Geri.

Geri Hudson Morgan

Foreword

By Dr. Bob Nichols

Joy and I met Dr. Elizabeth Vaughan over twenty-five years ago in Dallas, Texas. She had a large practice of ophthalmology in Dallas for forty years. When she was nineteen, her grandfather, a Methodist minister, told her she would be a "medical missionary."

When Dr. Vaughan consecrated her life to Jesus, she took off like an eagle to the Far East to share her medical expertise and the Gospel of Jesus Christ. She practiced medicine, taught surgery, and ministered God's love and power all over the world. Dr. Vaughan not only had a successful medical practice in Dallas, but God blessed her with a great humanitarian ministry to many poor and underprivileged people in China. God also used her to raise up a Christian television station based in Garland, Texas, which covered the Dallas/Ft. Worth Metroplex. I have admired Dr. Vaughan's great medical, humanitarian, and ministry achievements, as well as her ongoing commitment to Christ. She is a blessing to the body of Christ.

Dr. Vaughan has a passion for the fullness of Christ to be manifested in the lives of all believers, which is evident in her book, *Jesus Needs a Body*. This book will help and encourage every believer to understand how Jesus uses His body—the body of Christ—on the earth to carry out His work through us. The biblical principle that Jesus needs a body to speak through and to work through is a life-changing revelation. Romans 13:14 admonishes us to put on the Lord Jesus Christ. *Jesus Needs a Body* illustrates miracles in the Bible and many personal miracles in Dr. Vaughan's life and ministry. By faith, each one of us can be used of God to facilitate His miracle-working power.

Dr. Vaughan is a member in good standing at Calvary Cathedral International and is a constant source of encouragement to Joy, me, and our church. She ministers at Calvary and has a passion for Jesus, the Word, the end-time harvest, and revival! She is hungry for God!

I would encourage every believer who desires a greater anointing of Jesus in his or her life to read this book prayerfully and carefully.

Dr. Bob Nichols
Pastor, Calvary Cathedral International
Fort Worth, Texas

God's Champion

Dr. Elizabeth Vaughan

Is there not a cause? As David's keen senses prioritized the situation between Goliath and the army of Israel and armed with his past victories through God, David did not hesitate to offer himself a vessel for God's use and won an epic victory for the kingdom of God. Dr. Vaughan, small in stature but mighty in faith, has prioritized her life to offer herself as a willing vessel to win victories for the kingdom of God on both small and epic scales.

This book tracks an amazing set of footprints that go down a myriad of pathways where Dr. Vaughan has won epic victories in God's kingdom, such as choosing a medical career that brought better vision to thousands of eyes, such as establishing a center in Beijing, China, for free eye surgery, and such as creating a Christian television station for the Dallas/Ft. Worth Metroplex.

But also along this pathway are interesting turns like appearing on the Phil Donahue Show to validate a miracle by God, preaching a sermon in Jerusalem that answered a missionary's prayer, experiencing a divine appointment on the ancient wall of Xian, China, seeing a cripple transformed into a sprinter through her prayers in Cincinnati, meeting an angel in a subway in New York, and giving a tambourine to an orphan in Costa Rica. Today, she is still following where He leads, leaving footprints in all parts of the world, in all kinds of lives—including my own—to encourage others to become champions for His cause.

Gaye Savant, BFA
God's Servant

Kathryn Kuhlman Letter

The following was taken from a letter to Dr. Vaughan from Kathryn Kuhlman, dated January 8, 1975.

There is really <u>no limit</u> to what God can do with a person, providing that one will not touch the glory. God is still waiting for <u>one</u> who will be more fully devoted to Him than any who has ever lived; who will be willing to <u>be nothing</u> that Christ may be all; who will grasp God's own purposes and taking His humility and His faith, His love and His power—<u>without hindering, let</u> God do great things.

Kathryn Kuhlman

I have been meditating on the above paragraph for over forty years. It is one of the most impactful statements I have ever read—outside of the Bible. Its message has deeper and deeper meanings, the longer you think on it. It describes a person God is still waiting for. It could be <u>you</u>. **All Jesus needs is a body!**

Introduction

It is 4:40 p.m. on Thursday, January 19, 2017. About an hour ago, I arrived home from a trip to Thailand, traveling around 18,000 miles in nine days. On the plane coming home, the Lord showed me the outline for this book and dropped a desire in my heart to write it. He even gave me the name for the book, *Jesus Needs a Body*.

My friend, Dennis, picked me up from the airport, and on the way home, he said, "What are you going to do next?"

I said, "I am going to write another book."

To this he replied, "Are you going to name it *Jesus Needs a Body*?"

He said the same name that the Spirit had given me on the plane. I didn't really need confirmation, but I am grateful that God gave it to me anyway.

When I walked in the door of my home, I loved on my dogs and then sat down to go through the piles of mail that had accumulated during my absence. The Holy Spirit told me to stop doing that and come straight to the computer to start writing this book. I felt a real urgency through Him, and I always try my best to obey Him immediately. So here we go…

Two years ago, a friend gave me a little book about the 23rd Psalm, written by a real-life shepherd. Usually, I don't read any books except the Bible, but I felt led to read this one. I learned a great deal about sheep and shepherds, but more importantly, the Lord gave me a revelation about our lives as His sheep. I entitled this revelation "The Plateau of Promise."

Subsequent to that, the Lord put together a number of experiences of mine and others' and clearly showed me how He needs a body through which to function in this earthly realm. I entitled this revelation, "Jesus Needs a Body."

More recently, the Holy Spirit showed me a third revelation entitled, "Immersed in Jesus." These three revelations fit together like pieces of a puzzle. They have changed my thinking, my ministry, and my life. I hope they will change yours too. They comprise the heart of this book, surrounded by experiences from over forty-two years of ministry in many nations—dreams, visions, angel encounters, miracles, wonders, and a variety of additional revelations from God.

I want to preface all the stories about "miracles" in this book by giving you a Webster's Dictionary definition of a miracle: "an extraordinary event manifesting <u>divine intervention</u> in human affairs."

People often think of miracles as God parting the Red Sea or making someone see who was born blind or raising a dead person to life. Obviously, these are miracles, but we need to enlarge our understanding of miracles to things that happen in our lives that have no other explanation for them other than God's loving hand intervening.

Such are the true events I will relate to you in this book. They are all miracles I have seen or participated in personally. Nothing in this book is fiction. Everything is reality and truth. Maybe we need to open our spiritual eyes and give God credit for doing the astonishing, unexplainable, good things He does in our lives. Maybe we should finally recognize them as miracles from our Father who loves us.

Above all, I pray that this book helps you understand that Jesus needs a person to work through on this earth, and the person He wants is you. Be willing to give yourself into His hands just like you are. You don't have to wait until you are perfect. That would never happen. <u>He will be happy to be your partner for life and use you in ways you could never imagine.</u> **Jesus needs your body!**

Chapter 1

TV Miracles

Pursue

When the desire came into my heart to build a Christian TV station, I began investigating that possibility the best I knew how. It seemed like every door I knocked on was tightly closed, and after several months, I decided to "put it on the back burner." As an eye surgeon, I had a very busy and growing practice of medicine. New surgical devices and techniques had come out. I was very excited about them and actively involved in using them to better help patients. My life was very full. I did not need anything else to do, and yet with all my heart, I wanted to obey God. I was in a quandary as to whether to let the idea of the TV station go or pick up the baton again and chase after it.

One night, I went to church with this question in the forefront of my mind. I was asking God for His perfect will. I had determined to do nothing further until I was certain of His will concerning this matter. That night, a visiting evangelist, Francine Morrison, was ministering at our church. In the middle of her sermon, she stopped abruptly and said, "God has a word for someone here tonight." She turned to face my direction and said, "Pursue, and surely you will overcome and recover all" (1 Samuel 30:8). She then turned away and continued preaching her sermon, which was totally unrelated to the word she had just spoken. Her words went through me like an arrow. I knew God had given me His answer to my question about TV. His answer was unequivocally, "**PURSUE.**" And that is exactly what I did.

About this time, a patient came in and asked if I would do a new surgical procedure on him called Radial Keratotomy. I had heard about this technique at the American Academy of Ophthalmology meeting, but I had no interest in doing it. It involved making radial incisions on the cornea of the eye to correct nearsightedness. That meant you would be doing surgery on an eye that had no cataract or disease, which was a divergence from all thinking I had ever had about eye surgery. I told the young man I would not do the surgery. He went away dejected. In about six months, he returned and again asked me if I would do the surgery. Again I told him no. When he came back the third time, the Lord told me to investigate the procedure further.

I traveled to one of the rare places in America where it was being done and learned the details of the technique. The Lord instructed me to begin doing Radial Keratotomy. It was only in obedience to God that I was willing to do this surgery. I bought the needed instruments and equipment and began doing it. The first patient I did it on was the young man that had plead with me to do it. He was so elated by the results that the second patient to request it was his father.

Quickly, people started hearing about the results of no longer needing glasses after this surgery, and they started flooding into my office. I had so many people tell me that this was the greatest thing that had happened in their lives. One man told me that he went to the top of a hill and sat there all night just looking around. He was amazed at how he could see everything clearly at a distance, which he had never been able to do in his life without glasses.

I also remember a young woman who said she had been swimming at the seashore when a huge wave hit her in her face, knocking her glasses off. She was so blind without her glasses that she did not know which way the shore was. She was extremely frightened. After having the surgery, she could now see, and loved to go swimming in the ocean without fear.

The reason I am telling you about Radial Keratotomy is because God used the revenue generated from it to finance much of the building of the television station. If He hadn't told me to do the procedure, I would never have done it, and I would have lacked the funding to build the Christian TV station. God's ways are always so much higher than ours. He is so far ahead of us, planning steps to accomplish what He desires. He sees the end from the beginning. We usually have no idea why He is telling us to do certain things—like doing this new surgical technique. In retrospect, it was for the purpose of blessing so many people and, at the same time, helping to build His television station.

The following are some of the amazing miracles God did to accomplish the building of the TV station.

The Tower Miracle

When we were in the process of building a five-million-watt television station in the Dallas/Ft. Worth Metroplex, an absolutely essential part of the application to the FCC was an appropriate tower site. The first step in this process was to find a tower site that would be acceptable to the FAA. In a busy metroplex like Dallas/Ft. Worth, that was not an easy thing to do with planes coming and going from every direction into the multiple airports in the area. We obviously needed help to do this, so we hired FAA consultants that were experts in doing this very thing. They made all their searches and calculations and came up with a location north of Dallas that they felt was perfect for a tower site. Because of this expert advice, we began looking for some land in the location they had chosen. We did find a rancher that wanted to sell some land at that location, so we bought it.

Now that we had the site secured, we made application to the FAA for their permission to build the tower there. After many months of waiting, the anticipated answer came. We were totally shocked to find out that the FAA had DENIED our request. The consultants felt strongly that the FAA had made a mistake, since in their opinion, the site they had chosen was ideal. Their recommendation to us was to file an appeal. Of course, we had hired them for their expertise, so what were we to do but to follow their advice? The appeal was filed, and then we played the waiting game again. Meanwhile, the deadline for having our application to the FCC was drawing ever closer. We had to "get all our ducks in a row," and do it quickly. But the time the FAA would take to decide on the appeal was totally out of our control—so we waited.

Finally, the answer came...DENIED AGAIN. The consultants had failed. They could find no other site that they felt was appropriate. What were we to do? This seemed to be an impossible situation, like the one the children of Israel faced when the impassable Red Sea was in front of them, and the entire Egyptian army, with their chariots and men of war, was chasing them from behind. There was no way of escape except by a miracle. So it was with us at this point. All of our enormous efforts toward building a Christian television station would soon be "down the drain" without a tower site—and that was needed FAST!

The next place to go was on my knees, which is exactly what I did. I asked the Lord to do the impossible, and show me a tower site that would be acceptable to the FAA, a site that the experts said did not exist. Isn't the Lord wonderful? His ways are so much higher than ours, and there is NEVER a situation that is impossible to the CREATOR OF THE UNIVERSE. We think so small, and He thinks so big. Our vision is so limited, and His is infinite. Our love is so little, and His is limitless. What a glorious God we serve! Is anything too difficult for God? So I got out all the information that I had on the subject, including charts of flight patterns in the Dallas/ Ft. Worth area. I spread the charts on the floor because they were too large to fit on my desk, and I began to study them in great detail.

We had purchased two buildings in an industrial area in Garland, Texas, which were our proposed television station headquarters. As I poured over the charts, I noticed there was one tiny spot in this huge metroplex area that looked like it was outside all the flight pathways. This tiny spot was somewhere in Garland, so I got out a bigger map of Garland to pin point this tiny spot. Guess where it was? You guessed it. It was exactly at the location of our buildings. No one can do that but God!!

There was a fenced yard behind our buildings that turned out to be large enough to build a free-standing tower for our antenna. Once more, we made application to the FAA, this time for approval to use this new spot as our tower site. As usual, there was a wait, and our FCC deadline was now getting critically near. Finally, the decision came… "APPROVED." So we now had a tower site on which to build a tower seventy-eight stories tall, which we were told would be the tallest free-standing tower in Texas at the time. This was obviously a miracle supplied by the hand of our God.

Garland City Council

Now that we had FAA approval of our tower site, we needed the City of Garland to approve the building of the tower. The first step was to meet with the engineering committee and get their recommendation to the City Council. Geri and I were scheduled to be at a convention out of town at the time of this committee meeting, so we sent our chief engineer and our general manager (who was a veteran in the television world) to represent us at this very important meeting. We felt confident that they would be able to get a stamp of approval for our project. When the committee's decision came out, we got a phone call that was totally unexpected. The committee was going to recommend that the City Council NOT allow the building of our tower.

We were all in shock. At church the next Sunday, my pastor got a word from God for me. It was to "use the gift He had put within me." I had no idea what he was talking about. After church, I asked the pastor what God meant, and he replied, "The gift of faith." So I put all my faith in God to resolve this situation in our favor, and so did everyone else who was involved. We all joined together with our focus solely on Him. Jesus was our only hope!

The day of the City Council meeting was set, and it happened to be only a few days before our FCC deadline to file the completed application for the television station. Everything was at stake. We would either get their approval on that day or totally lose the television station. It was an evening meeting, and there was a crowd there. First, the engineering committee gave their recommendation—DO NOT allow the building of the tower. Then any neighbors or citizens of Garland could give their opinions. One by one they came to the microphone saying comments AGAINST the building of the tower. "It might fall down on our buildings nearby." "Ice might form on the tower in the winter and fall off, damaging our cars or our property." Thus the parade of negative opinions continued.

When they had all made their thoughts known, the council called for any positive opinions. I was the only person to speak in favor of building the tower. My heart was pounding. This was it...now or never. I can't remember exactly what I said, but I'm sure it was everything I could think of.

The council took a short recess with me still standing in front of the microphone. They came back and said that since so many people were against it, they had come up with the idea of a small piece of land by the railroad tracks where they would permit the building of the tower instead of putting it on our property. Alarm bells went off inside of me. I immediately responded that the FAA had approved our proposed tower site and that the FCC deadline was eminent. There was no time to try to get a different tower site approved by the FAA. If they didn't approve the building of the tower RIGHT NOW, the government's station allocation to Garland, Texas, would go back to Richardson, Texas, where it was originally allocated. Garland would then lose FOREVER its ability to have a television station.

Well, that scenario set them on their heels, and they took another short break. When they returned, it was time to vote. Each council member had a button in front of them where they could either vote yes or no. Whichever way they voted would be shown on a light panel in front of the entire audience. The moment had arrived. One by one the votes were seen by us all...YES-YES-YES-YES, etc. Every vote was affirmative. GOD HAD WON AGAIN!! We had seen another miracle.

Permission to build the tower on our own property was granted. Now we were ready to go to the FCC and try to win the construction permit, which was the permission to build and own this station. This was the last channel allocated to the Dallas/Ft. Worth Metroplex by the federal government, and therefore, it was highly sought after. Only God could bring this to pass.

The FCC Hearing

Once the Lord told me to "pursue" building a Christian TV station in the Dallas/Ft. Worth Metroplex, I put my whole effort into it. This was in the 1980s, before the advent of satellite TV, which is now filled with Christian programing. I had no idea what was involved in this and what an arduous task it would be. But in my mind, if God said to do it, you just did it, knowing that He would make a way where there seemed to be no way. We do serve a God of miracles, and nothing is too difficult for Him!

I will not go into all the details of every step, but I want to relate something amazing that took place at the FCC hearing for the station in Washington, D.C. There was another group trying to get the station in addition to us. It was a large company that owned several other TV stations across America.

Obviously, they had a great deal of experience, and we had none. There were three attorneys present at the hearing, the attorney for the opposing company, an attorney representing "the people," and our attorney.

There were four ladies going on this trip to Washington, Geri (the vice president of our company), Melinda (the secretary of our company), an assistant, and myself. We had decided to fly to New York first, since two of the ladies had never been there, and drive to Washington, D.C. the next day. Melinda and I had been studying diligently for the hearing and continued doing so that night in New York. After much study, Geri decided that it was impossible for her to know the voluminous stacks of detailed information about the station and, therefore, went out sight-seeing with her assistant that evening, having a good time. She was clinging to the scripture, "…take no thought how or what ye shall speak: for it shall be given you that same hour what ye shall speak" (Matt.10:19). Of course, we had all prayed that the Lord would help us; we knew He was our only hope of getting the station.

On the morning of the hearing, I was called to the stand first since I was the president of the company. The opposing attorney began to grill me about every aspect of the TV station, antenna pattern, engineering, demographics, etc. The questioning continued until lunch and then resumed afterwards.

After many hours of his questions and my correct answers (by the grace of God), the attorney finally asked me a question I did not have an answer for. I hesitated a moment, trying to think of the answer. As I began to say, "I don't know," I had just gotten the "I" out of my mouth when the "people's attorney" spoke up and said, "She obviously did …," and he gave the answer. The judge looked at me and asked if that was correct, and I quickly answered in the affirmative. God had intervened through this attorney who had not said one word all day and did not say another word for the rest of the day.

More questions ensued, which I answered. By this time, it was late afternoon, and I think the attorney was exhausted, so he let me go. As I took my seat, our attorney handed me a note, which I cherish. I have it in a frame on the wall of my study. He wrote, "<u>Tremendous</u>! One of the few cases in my recollection where the witness forgot <u>nothing</u>." Of course, no one but God knew that I really could not have answered one of the questions without the help of the Holy Spirit using the "people's attorney."

Next, he called Geri to the stand. He asked her name…she knew the answer. Then he asked her address…again she knew the answer. So far, she was doing well. He asked her date of birth and a few other simple questions about her life that were very easy for her to answer. He was looking at a biography that each one of us had to provide, and he said, "I see that you were a member of the Dad's Club." Geri answered, "No sir, I just played the piano for the Dad's Club." He was so humiliated by his silly question and her answer that he immediately excused her from the stand without a single question about the TV station. She had "dodged the bullet," and just like in my case, it was by the grace of God.

Now it was Melinda's turn. There was very little time left. The attorney asked her some brief questions about the TV station, which she answered correctly. Five o'clock came quickly, and the hearing ended. How relieved we all were to have that ordeal behind us.

On the day of the hearing, we had tried to call our good friend, Ruth Ward Heflin, to see if there was any possibility for her to come and be with us. She was away on a trip and not at home. She was a powerful woman of God, and we coveted her prayers. Of all the places in the world where she could have been, we discovered that she was already in Washington, D.C., led there by the Holy Spirit to be with us. She sat nearby and prayed for us throughout the hearing. He answers before we call. What an amazing God we serve!

The outcome of the hearing granted us the construction permit, which meant the station allocation was ours. Now we had to build it, which required another series of miracles.

I want to share something funny that happened while I was in our FCC attorney's office in Washington, D.C. This happened several months prior to the hearing I just described.

It was during the time that I was doing television programs and was wearing false eyelashes, which were placed on one lash at a time. Geri said I looked like Bambi, but I got many compliments on them. Actually, they were a nuisance because every morning I had to replace every lash that had fallen out during the prior twenty-four hours.

At this meeting, Jim Gammon, our attorney, had papers spread out all over his desk, and he was showing me things about our FCC application. It was a very formal setting. As I was leaning over his desk intently studying the information, an eyelash fell out—right in the middle of his important papers. It was very visible. What would you have done? (I am speaking to the ladies now.)

Well, I quickly reached down, brushed it off of his papers, and never said a word about it. He kept on talking as though it had never happened. Maybe he had never seen a false eyelash and had no idea what it was. I was serious on the outside, but laughing on the inside!

Chapter 2

Experiences

Meeting Geri

A friend asked me the other day how I met Geri Morgan. That has been a question frequently asked since God has used us together over the years. Therefore, I thought I would tell you the story so you wouldn't wonder.

As a young doctor, a patient who was working with Campus Crusade for Christ came in to see me. While there, he asked if I would help support him, and I agreed to do so. Consequently, I began getting literature from Campus Crusade. One day, I got a flyer about a "spiritual enrichment" meeting at Lake Texoma. I thought that I could use some spiritual enrichment, so I signed up for it. That meeting was a life-changing experience.

There, I was introduced to the *Four Spiritual Laws* booklet, which explained that there was a throne in your life, determining who was in control of your life. If you were on the throne, your life would grow fruit like discontent, frustration, anger, discouragement, etc. If you asked Jesus to be on the throne of your life (i.e. in control of your life), then He would grow things like love, joy, peace, patience, gentleness, kindness, faith, etc.

Well, it didn't take an M.D. degree to figure out what kind of life I would rather have! How strange that I had been reared in the church, taken there every time the doors opened by a mother consecrated to God, and yet, I never knew that you could give your life to God. At any rate, I quickly made that decision. I felt that a quality decision like I had made needed to have some "teeth to it," some outward action brought about by the inward commitment.

I knew that God had said, "Seek ye first the kingdom of God, and his righteousness, and all these things shall be added unto you," (Matt. 6:33). I also knew that He magnified His word above His name (Ps. 138:2). So to show God that I was serious about seeking Him first, I decided to begin reading my Bible early, every morning. Even though I had read the Bible all my life, it now came alive. I was so interested in what the Lord was showing me in His Word that I would set my alarm clock earlier and earlier every morning to have more time to read it. I was almost getting up at the same time I went to bed. It was so exciting to me! What a difference this sincere decision had made in my life.

I also got Campus Crusade literature called the *Nine Transferable Concepts*. One of those concepts was about the Holy Spirit. I had known virtually nothing about the Holy Spirit until that time. I only knew that we said, "In the name of the Father, the Son, and the Holy Spirit." I had no clue about who He is or His function in our lives. This booklet changed that. I learned that He is our teacher and would lead us into all truth. He is the Third Person of the Godhead that is with us on the earth right now. He is our Comforter and our Helper. Actually, He is someone we cannot live without if we want to draw close to God and have His power flow through us.

Jesus said, in Acts 1:8, "But ye shall receive <u>power</u> afte
Ghost is come upon you: and ye shall be witnesses unto
uttermost part of the earth." So, He is the <u>power</u> of God th
to live within any child of God.

How do you receive this Person of the Holy Spirit? The booklet qu
the words of Jesus. "If a son shall ask bread of any of you that is a father, will
he give him a stone? or if he ask a fish, will he for a fish give him a serpent?
… If ye then, being evil, know how to give good gifts unto your children:
how much more shall your heavenly Father give the Holy Spirit to them
that ask him?" (Luke 11:11, 13). There was the answer. As a child of God
(i.e. saved, born again), all I had to do was simply <u>ask</u>.

I knelt alone in my living room and asked God to fill me with the Holy
Spirit. I didn't see any flashing lights or hear angels singing or any other
supernatural phenomenon. I simply believed that I had received what I
asked for because that was God's promise to me. I did not know that Jesus
referred to this experience as being "baptized with the Holy Ghost" (Acts
1:5) because the booklet made no mention of that terminology. I discovered that for myself later.

That experience totally changed my life. I caught on fire for God. I got
some friends together and wanted to go through the "transferable concepts" with them. I don't think they had much interest, but I was so enthusiastic that they went along with me. I couldn't get enough of the things
of God. I was starved for more of Him, and I was excited beyond words. I
prayed and asked God to give me a friend who knew more about the things
of the Spirit than I did. Shortly, He led me to a meeting where I met an
older woman. She had been operating in the Holy Ghost a long time, and
she took me to meetings where the gifts of the Spirit were in operation (1
Cor. 12:7-11).

She kept telling me that she had another friend about my age who had
been helping her in ministry, and she wanted me to meet her. She said we
would become good friends because we both had a deep love for the Lord.

months passed before I actually met this friend, who was Geri. I met her very briefly while taking her and my older friend to the airport one morning. Geri was busy talking to someone on the phone, so I had no time to get to know her.

The next Sunday morning, I decided to visit Tyler Street Methodist Church, where I had heard there was a good move of the Spirit at that time. The pastor read the passage of scripture where Jesus sent seventy of His followers out two by two to reap the harvest and heal the sick (Luke 10). At that moment, the Holy Spirit said to me, "I am sending Geri out with you—two by two." I was shocked. I didn't even know Geri, but I knew the voice of the Spirit had spoken.

When Geri returned from the trip, we had our first conversation. We discovered that we had nothing in common in the natural. She was a professional musician, and I was a doctor. She liked thrift stores and garage sales, and I liked the out of doors. Despite our differences, we both had the same intense heart for God. That was the beginning of a lifelong friendship and a lifetime of traveling the nations in the name of Jesus. Just as the Holy Spirit had spoken to me, He sent us out two by two to fulfill His purposes… and what a journey it has been!

Russia

In the fall of 1982, a small group of us decided to go to Russia to encourage believers behind the Iron Curtain and, if possible, to share the good news of Jesus Christ with those who had never heard it. We flew from New York to Vienna, Austria, and there rented a Volkswagen van. It happened to be chartreuse in color, which did nothing to help the secrecy of our mission!

We loaded it to full capacity with eight of us packed inside like sardines, and all of our luggage strapped on the top. We cheerfully headed across Austria, Czechoslovakia, and Poland toward the western border of Russia with high hopes of being able to accomplish our purpose there. If we had had any inkling of what awaited us, we wouldn't have been nearly so cheerful.

The countryside was very beautiful in Poland. We stopped in Zakopane, where the local men were carving wooden platters with scenes of their country surrounded by bright colored borders. They were so pretty that we bought several, and I still have them hanging in my home as a reminder of that wonderful spot.

As our trip continued across Poland, we visited Auschwitz, where four million Jews were killed by Hitler. It was beyond comprehension how the human mind could conceive of the atrocities committed against these people. It is extremely clear that these actions could have only been inspired by Satan and his demon forces. How could any human being have gone along with such hellish actions? It is hard to understand.

We saw rooms full of eye glasses and shoes of all sizes, even some belonging to small children. These were articles taken from those murdered. We saw lamp shades made from human skin. There were pictures of human experiments where body parts had been surgically attached to other body parts where they did not belong, presumably just to see what would happen—with no regard for the suffering this imposed on the recipients. Of course, there was the crematorium where a continual train of bodies were burned, with billowing clouds of putrid smoke pouring from their stacks night and day. Gas chambers existed, where the room would be filled with people, and then poisonous gas spewed into the room, killing everyone. In retrospect, that seems like a merciful end compared to what happened to those still living. Only God knows the agony of body and soul that went on in that "hell on earth."

After that heart-wrenching experience, we reached the heavily guarded Russian border at night. Soldiers were standing around us with guns. Over loud speakers, they were broadcasting intimidating sounds of wolves howling and people screaming in agony as they were being tortured. It was not a place where anyone would choose to be! They made us get out of the vehicle and then proceeded to tear the van apart piece by piece, even looking between the pieces of metal in the body of it with some instrument like a periscope. I was bold enough to ask what they were looking for. The answer was unclear, but it was obvious they thought we were bringing in something that was banned. If they could have examined our hearts, they would have found out the answer.

We were bringing in love to our oppressed brothers and sisters, and hope which only Jesus can provide. These things they could not take away from us. After four to five hours of searching and finding no contraband, they reassembled our van, and we continued driving into the Ukraine at night.

It was late at night when we reached our hotel. I had never seen any hotel in America or any other part of the world like this one. The building was very old, the ceilings were high, and the light so dim you could hardly see your hand in front of your face. We checked in and were led down a pitch black corridor until someone turned on what appeared to be a ten-watt light bulb at the top of the twenty-foot ceiling.

No "haunted house" could ever be this creepy. We had been warned that everything, everywhere in Russia, could be "bugged"—the tables where we would eat, the bedrooms where we would sleep, even the car we were driving. With this in mind, we entered our small, dim hotel room. We couldn't discuss the events of the day or anything else, so we both decided to read before turning off the tiny light and going to sleep. Geri chose to read some literature she had picked up at Auschwitz describing further atrocities from hell. I chose to read my Bible. When the lights went off, I had sound sleep. Geri, on the other hand, had dreams in keeping with the book she had been reading. The devil pervaded her dreams with nightmares about her daughter and other loved ones being tortured, etc.

The next morning, she was definitely ready to go home on the next flight out. Of course, that was not possible, so we crawled back into the chartreuse van and continued going deeper into Russia. She said she was counting the days and the hours until she could leave communist Russia.

The only souvenir that Geri kept from that creepy hotel was a small piece of toilet paper, which I later found in her scrap book. It measured two inches in width and was beige with faded brown stripes. I guess it was in keeping with everything else about that place.

Geri and I wandered away from the group one day and stopped to visit a bakery. There were some women employees that were friendly to us and started communicating with us the best that they could with the language barrier. The police were called because the workers were being friendly with us, so we left.

We next found a department store and went in. Since Geri loves to shop, she was now in her element. She was interested in buying some little wooden, matrioska dolls, where one figure fits inside a larger figure. There are usually several of these stacked inside one another. Since she couldn't speak the language, she drew a little picture to show the sales lady what she was looking for. The picture looked almost exactly like Casper the Ghost, but somehow the lady understood and proudly took us to the dolls.

On the 25th of September, we were in Kiev, and it was Geri's birthday. I asked her what she would like for her birthday, and she said she wanted Chicken Kiev for dinner—since we were in Kiev. We went to a nice restaurant, and when we tried to order Chicken Kiev, the waiter said he had never heard of this dish. As strange as it may seem, you can't get Chicken Kiev in Kiev! We would have to wait on that birthday meal until we got home to America.

Women on the street would stop me and try to buy the shoes and dresses I was wearing. The clothes were quite ordinary, but to them they were wonderful. Of course, I couldn't disrobe on the street and let them have my clothes, but I would have been willing to bless them with the clothes if I could have. They would always approach with caution and secrecy, as if afraid of being seen by the police talking to a foreigner. I have no idea what would have happened to them, but I do know they seemed afraid. Our group was able to bless believers with some musical instruments, blue jeans and far more importantly, the message that we cared about them and were praying for them. They were not alone.

One of the memorable experiences in ministry was a night when I was invited to preach at a church in Russia. I wore a scarf over my head, as was the custom, and shared through an interpreter what the Holy Spirit had put on my heart. That entire service, though done in secrecy, was recorded, and I was given a copy of it, which would become important in our later travels in Russia. The Lord knows the end from the beginning and often does things for reasons beyond our understanding at the time.

As our time in Russia came to an end, we approached the border crossing once more. This time, the exit ordeal was greater than the entrance ordeal. They again disassembled the van, examining every inch with x-rays and every other method they could devise. Of course, they found nothing because there was nothing there to be found. They took all our possessions away from us and went through every tiny scrap of paper in our purses and our luggage. This took many hours. They found a small audio player in my luggage that had the recording of the church service with me preaching. They confiscated it after listening to it. Now they had all heard the gospel, and they could never stand before the throne of God and say they had never heard of His Son, Jesus, who died for their sins. Hopefully one of the soldiers would take it home to secretly share it with family and friends. That cassette recording was God's "plant" for His purposes.

While they were tearing the van apart, they separated the men from the women and paraded us into a building. What in the world would they do to us next? I was the first woman in line. The big, tough-looking female soldiers commanded me to remove my shoes, which I did. They then commanded me to put them back on, which I did. They then commanded me to move on. I had no idea what they were doing to the women behind me. Later, I found out that they were strip-searching everyone else in the party.

Geri came after me in the line, and they made her remove everything. I mean <u>everything</u>, including her wig, which she never took off under any circumstances. She would even go swimming with the wig on. I think being "wigless" was more humiliating to her than being "clothesless." So after eleven hours at this border crossing, they had seen everything we had—literally. We were tired, hungry, and exhausted, yet so relieved to be free again. We traveled back to Vienna via Budapest, Hungary. We had put twenty-six hundred miles on that little chartreuse van by the time we returned it to the rental company.

Geri vowed that she would never go back there and live through hell again, unless God specifically told her to do so. When our plane finally landed on American soil again, she fell on her knees and kissed the tarmac. What an adventure we had had!

Geri, Dr. Vaughan, Russian lady
(Lvov, Russia - September 1982).

The Emergency Room

Part of being on a hospital staff is covering the emergency room on a rotating schedule with other doctors in your specialty. So as an eye surgeon for many years, I had seen many emergencies and cared for them according to their needs. I had seen just about every kind of eye trauma you could imagine.

On this particular night, I was called to the emergency room of a hospital that had a large volume of trauma cases. I was told that the man they had called me to see had been in a bad auto accident. That description did not prepare me for his actual condition. I hate to be too graphic with you, but his head was like a watermelon that had fallen off of the back of a truck and was broken open. The fact that his eyes were damaged was the least of his problems. He was on a breathing machine, and they were working feverishly to keep him alive. I examined his eyes and wondered why they had called me. It was obvious that he could not live with the severe injuries he had sustained.

After accessing his eye status, I went upstairs to the wards to see other patients with other eye problems. I remember pausing and looking out a window into the dark. I felt an urgency to pray for this man's soul while he was still alive. I knew he had only a few more minutes in this world before he would meet his Maker, and I didn't feel in my spirit that he was prepared for that. I asked the Lord to forgive his sins and give him a chance, even in his comatose condition, to choose Jesus as his Savior. A peace came over me, and I knew that by God's grace he had been saved.

After I finished seeing patients on the wards, I went back down to the emergency room and found John dead, with his wife by his side. She said words I will never forget. She said to the body, "Oh John, you are so <u>cold</u>." She was weeping. This whole thing was a total shock to her. When he left for work that day, he was well and healthy. He was in his forties with no thoughts whatsoever of dying that day. He had been going too fast in a sports car and lost control, wrapping his car around a light pole. Suddenly, she became a widow. Her words still ring in my ears, reminding me to appreciate every day with everyone that I care about and to thank God that they are still <u>warm</u>.

I interrupted her grieving long enough to tell her who I was and that I knew John was saved. She seemed too distressed to pay much attention to what I had said. The one who was rejoicing at my prayer for him was John in heaven. I believe John's salvation was the only reason that I was called to the hospital emergency room that night. It was not for John's eyes; it was for his soul.

God has amazing ways of accomplishing His purposes, even if no one knows about it but you and God. The Lord is "not willing that any should perish, but that <u>all</u> should come to repentance" (2 Peter 3:9). God has enormous love for us and wants every one of us to accept Jesus as our Lord and Savior so that we can spend eternity in heaven with Him.

The Ron Martin Story—Lessons from the Edge of Death

On September 8, 2016, Ron's wife died. The next day Ron's daughter, Krista, received a phone call from the doctor that her dad was a very sick man. She rushed him to the hospital where they discovered he was severely anemic among other things. They gave him two pints of blood immediately, and as quickly as prudent, they took him to surgery. For several days after this, he was hanging in a place between life and death. He had no memory of anything that happened during the first 2-3 days, but after that, he felt that he was going to die, and he was in a very different world.

As he lay in his hospital room, he had bizarre visions of things flying around. He wanted to get up to heaven, but he felt panic because of the place where he envisioned himself to be. He tried in many ways to have people pull him out of this imagined place or lift him up from there, but all attempts failed. He thought water was going to fall on him and drown him in this dismal place.

The devil came to him, and said, "I'm here to get you." He had "horns straight like teeth sticking out by his mouth, a black face, black clothes, and was ugly." A red light was turned on by the devil's side, and as long as that light was on, Ron knew he could not go to heaven. He started repenting of everything he could think of. That seemed to make the devil go away for a while, and then he would come back.

For 48 hours, Ron talked continually to the Lord with his eyes wide open, repenting of things he could remember throughout his life. He saw angels and heard them singing beautifully. He saw a door above him as he walked on "shiny, beautiful steps." There was a woman standing in the door who he thought was his recently deceased wife. He wanted so badly to go there, but something was pulling him back. He was frustrated that he was not leaving, yet he felt "it wasn't his time yet."

So this see-saw between heaven and the devil continued during the 48 hours that he continually talked to the Lord and repented. There was a white light to his right that never came on. He knew that when the white light did come on, he would be ready to go to heaven. The Lord kept telling him, "There is one more thing." He went back over every person in his whole life that he could think of that had not already been mentioned in repentance, but the Lord still said, "There is one more thing."

Finally, Ron thought of his dad who had been an alcoholic and a gambler. He had never done anything offensive to his dad or said anything offensive about his dad, but in his heart, he held wrong feelings against him for the things he had done to the family. When Ron repented for these negative thoughts, the white light went on, and he knew he was finally free from all sin he had committed. The devil's red light now went off. Ron said, "He never got me because I repented, and I had no reason to go with him."

Suddenly, Ron came more fully to himself in the hospital room. Besides talking to the Lord, he was only able to say his name and birthdate or occasionally say yes or no. Other than that, he had been virtually unresponsive during the previous 48 hours. They had given him the strongest sleeping medicine they had, and still he would not sleep. He just kept on talking to the Lord and telling about heaven and other things he was seeing. After he came to himself, the doctor asked him why he wasn't sleeping. He replied, "I can't. The Lord won't let me, and I have to listen to what He has to say."

As soon as he awakened from this experience, he was completely coherent. He asked the nurses to leave the room, for he wanted to talk to Krista in private. He told her that he knew he was going to live, and he asked if he could come and live with her family. She gladly consented.

After this experience, Ron reflected on his spiritual life. "I went to church as a little kid, but a lot of times, it was just to make Mom happy. But now I go because I want to go." In the last 35 to 40 years before this experience, he and his wife missed church very few times. "It was uplifting for the day and helped us get going for the week." Yet in his heart, "I always thought a tough guy didn't need God, and I was a tough guy."

Now he says, "I decided the tough guy needed God more than the weak guy." Before this experience, Ron assumed that he would go right to heaven when he died. How many people warming the church pews on a regular basis think the same way? How many of them are wrong as Ron was?

I asked Ron what he would say if he met an old friend now. He answered, "'You'd better quit doing what you've been doing, and start talking to the Lord, and get repented.' See what the Lord wanted him to do; that there are better things for him than what he's been doing. He has to convince himself that he needs the Lord. Sometimes, it's not the easiest thing to do. To me, in times past, I would think I know as much about Him as they do." He had told some men that have "lady friends," "You know some of these days it might happen to you"...well it did.

I asked him, "The only way to get to heaven is what?"

He said, "Be honest with the Lord. Follow the Lord all the way through. You got to repent first. All the bad stuff (smoking, drinking, swearing, complaining about other people), get it out of your mind. Quit thinking about it. Live your life the best you can, and do what's right. Follow the Lord."

I said, "You learned that the **thoughts** you had were sins in the eyes of the Lord, not just what you did or what you said, but actually what you thought."

"That is right," he replied. "I have no desire for another lady now. I look at them, but I don't think nothing. I don't think they are pretty. I don't think they are fat or ugly. They are just ladies. If you get to thinking they are a big, fat lady, well that is wrong. Everybody has a soul. You get all kinds of people, but they are all good people, and you've got to respect that regardless of their race or whatever."

"It sounds like you've gotten your thoughts purified," I commented.

He said, "I hope so. That's what I'm working on."

While reflecting on the interview I had with Ron, two things stand out. The first is the fact that a wrong **thought** or attitude was keeping him out of heaven. Most serious Christians try to control their actions, and hopefully even their words, but how many even consider having pure thoughts? God has many things to say about this. Here are a few.

"<u>Do not judge</u> so that you will not be judged. For in the way you judge, you will be judged; and by your standard of measure, it shall be measured to you" (Matt. 7:1-2 NASB).

"You have heard that it was said, *You shall not commit adultery*; but I say to you that every one who looks at a woman to lust for her has committed adultery with her already <u>in his heart</u>" (Matt. 5:27-28 NASB).

"Finally brethren, whatsoever things are true, whatsoever things are honest, whatsoever things are just, whatsoever things are pure, whatsoever things are lovely, whatsoever things are of good report; if there be any virtue, and if there be any praise, **think** <u>on these things</u>." (Phil. 4:8 KJV) "Let your mind dwell on these things" (NASB).

"We are destroying speculations (imaginations) and every lofty thing raised up against the knowledge of God, and we are taking every **thought** captive to the obedience of Christ" (2 Cor. 10:5 NASB).

It behooves us all to learn this lesson of refusing judgmental or negative thoughts about others before we face the One who judges us. We will be judged in the same way we have judged others!

The second thing that stood out to me was the fact that Ron assumed he would go to heaven when he died. This assumption was wrong... Why? God says, "For God so loved the world, that he gave his only begotten Son, that whosoever **believeth in him** should not perish, but have everlasting life" (John 3:16).

The word "believe" means *to trust in, to rely on, and to cling to*. It does not mean merely to have mental assent. Too many people have intellectual knowledge that Jesus is the Son of God (the devils know this too), but they have not made Him the Lord of their lives. They do not cling to Him and rely on Him. Usually, they cling to and rely on themselves, their spouses, their jobs, their money or other things besides God.

Ron and his wife went to church. They even had Bible studies in their home—which is more than most Christians do. However, Ron honestly revealed what was in his heart: "I always thought a tough guy didn't need God, and I was a tough guy." His heart was obviously not clinging to Jesus and relying on Jesus. God knows the thoughts and intentions of our hearts. He judges by what is in our hearts, not by outward appearances. You can fool people most of the time, but you can NEVER fool God, and He is the judge.

I point this out not as an indictment against Ron, for I think he is an upright man who now loves God with all his heart. I respect him greatly for telling us the truth, so we can benefit from his mistakes. I point this out so that it can save some people from going to hell when they mistakenly think that going to church will get them into heaven. Church attendance is not the key to heaven. Repenting, loving Jesus, and serving Him with your whole heart is the key to heaven. Let us all thank Ron Martin for opening our eyes to what pleases God. Hopefully, we will all get to meet Ron in heaven—where I am sure he will be.

Ron Martin

Africa

I was invited to speak at a Christian conference in South Africa. Geri went with me, along with two assistants. I will share with you some of the spiritual and "not so spiritual" highlights of that trip.

First of all, the conference was great. The praise and worship was especially good. In fact, I can still remember one of the songs we sang even though it happened many years ago. I guess it is because we sang it repeatedly and with great vigor. The words were, "Fear not, fear not, for I am with you. Fear not, fear not, for I am with you, saith the Lord." Everyone danced around with great joy as we sang of God's faithful presence and protection.

A life-changing event took place one day when the pastor's daughter took Geri and me out to the Zulu area. There we met the Zulu witch doctor, standing by his small hut. He was wearing something like leather shorts with flaps in the front and back. He was bare-chested, except for a leather strap diagonally across his chest. His hair was greased with some unknown substance and had beads in it. He smelled like something foul and unearthly. I never smelled anything like it before or after that day.

The woman who took us there spoke to him in the Zulu language a few minutes, and then the witch doctor came quickly over to me and fell on his knees before me. I couldn't communicate with him, but I certainly could communicate with God for him. I asked God to reveal Himself to this man and to save him, his wife, and all the people he influenced. I really believed in my heart that God heard and answered that prayer, making this witch doctor and his wife powerful witnesses for Jesus among the Zulus.

Dr. Vaughan with Zulu witch doctor.

When I get to heaven, I expect to see him there, looking and smelling a lot better. After we left him, I asked why he had come over and knelt down before me. She said that she had told him that I was a powerful woman who was a representative of God. I have no idea what was in his mind after that comment, but I do believe it had the effect of leading him to Jesus.

I was the speaker that night at the convention. I went home from my visit to the Zulus and washed my hair and showered thoroughly, but nothing I could do made the smell of the witch doctor go away. It was terrible. I'm sure it was some potion he had concocted with ingredients I don't ever want to know about. That night, I shared my experience with the congregation. They rejoiced with me about the salvations, but they laughed and laughed about the odor. It wasn't funny to me. Maybe they knew something I did not know about those concoctions the Zulu witch doctor used.

After a wonderful time in God during the convention, we decided to see some of the local sites, and take advantage of being in Africa. One of the places we went was the Kimberly Diamond Mines. Geri wanted no part of going straight down into the dark interior of the earth to see how diamonds were mined. I wanted to see everything about everything, so down I went. It was very interesting, as I saw them blast out huge amounts of earth and put it on a conveyor belt that had an oily substance attached to it. The dirt would fall off, but the diamonds would stick to the oily surface. They probably do it in a more sophisticated way now, but when I was there, that is how they explained it to me. They gave me a small core of material that had not been broken. I still have it, and who knows, maybe there is a world class diamond hidden inside. The chances would probably be one in several trillion. No one knows but God.

We decided to go to Zimbabwe and see African animals in the wild. We flew to Victoria Falls in an airplane that was so small you thought it might need to flap its wings to get off the ground. The turbulence during the entire flight was something you would never want to experience again, but in the end, it was all worth it to see the beauty of those falls.

When we arrived, Geri wore a safari outfit including a hat. She went into some tall bushes to pose for a picture in her outfit. Shortly after that, a park ranger came by, and Geri asked him if there were any cobras or big snakes in the area. She always asked about snakes wherever we were in the world because she was petrified of them. He told her they did have snakes in that area. She asked him where they were, and he pointed to the bushes that she had just come out of, where she had her picture made. She almost fainted and wanted to leave that area immediately. I was sure glad we had seen the falls before she found out about the snakes!

Geri in her safari outfit at Victoria Falls.

We then went to an area that had wild game and checked into a small hotel. In the hotel lobby, there was a sign offering a trip to the heart of animal country with one night in a tree house. That sounded exciting, so we signed up to go the next day. They drove us by jeep to a remote area where the animals roamed freely. We got there at dusk and were assigned tree houses for the night. By "tree houses," they meant small wooden floors, built about three stories up in tall trees. The tree house had siding about three feet high with no screening above it. You had to climb up a very tall ladder and crawl through a hole in the floor of your "house" to get into it. Inside, there were two small beds—no water, no toilet, no electricity, no light. In fact, nothing else was in there but the beds.

The only toilet was a short walk through the bushes where they had killed a boa constrictor the night before. Do you think Geri would go there in a thousand years? NO! They gave each person a little candle, not much bigger than the one you would put on a birthday cake. They told us not to use much of it that night because they would wake us up with a loud horn very early in the morning before the sun came up. We would need the candle to see our way around our floor without falling three stories down through the hole in the floor to our death. (They didn't say it quite like that, but that is what they meant.)

Night came, and we climbed up our ladders to our "floor house." There were no stars or moon that night, so the only light we had at all was from our birthday candles. Geri had visions of boa constrictors crawling into our "house" during the night and doing what they do to people. She was terrified. She called out to the other two women who were in their tree for the night. She yelled, "Come over here, and stay with us." They yelled back, "NO!"

I offered to read to her to take her mind off of the dangerous animals of the night, which she thought would soon eat her for dinner. So I started reading the only book I had brought on this safari. It happened to be about jungle animals and how big they were, etc. Needless to say, that was not helpful. It was getting late, and since she had refused to put out our birthday candles, we now had the last few seconds of flickering flames, and then total darkness fell. I went to sleep. I have no idea what Geri did.

The next thing I heard was the blaring of the horn to wake us up. It was still pitch black dark as the tour guide had warned us it would be. Now, we had no candle light at all because ours had been totally spent the night before. We were feeling around on the floor, trying to find our things without falling through the hole in the floor. We finally vacated our "house," and Geri vowed never to return. And we had paid money to do this?

One of the women with us had made it down to the ground from her "house," but the other one was still sitting on the bed—afraid to come down the long ladder backwards. We had to get her down. She could not stay there forever. So I climbed up the ladder to her "house," persuaded her to come to the hole in the floor, and put one foot on the ladder. I then instructed her to look up and <u>never</u> to look down. I would be right there with her, and we would put one foot down the ladder at a time. I would touch her foot and guide it to the next rung and continue talking to her, telling her she was doing a good job. Slowly, we descended without her fainting. Thank God, we could now go look for animals instead of imagining them.

We did see a giraffe, kneeling at the waterhole to get a drink, water buffalo, and other hoofed animals. We came across a big, bull elephant that was swaying back and forth and seemed to be having some hormonal issues when we arrived. He did not look happy! Geri proceeded to bang on the side of the vehicle and make loud noises at him. I told her to please be quiet as he looked like he had the potential of tearing our little vehicle apart with great ease. She didn't seem to recognize the gravity of the situation.

We survived the safari and the night in the tree house. I consider it one of the most memorable experiences we have ever had. I thank God for letting my eyes see those beautiful animals in their natural habitat. I also thank Him for saving the Zulu witch doctor and his people. The trip to Africa had been fruitful and exciting. I look forward to the time God sends me there again.

Chapter 3

Revelations

Look OVER Goliath's Head

As I sat in a meeting during praise and worship, the Lord showed me that the entire army of Israel was looking at Goliath, who was about 9'10" tall, and not one soldier wanted to fight him because he was so huge. Fear was in their hearts because of what they <u>saw</u> with their eyes.

Years before, the Lord had said to me, "How many soldiers would have volunteered to fight Goliath if he had been 4'10" instead of 9'10"?" Of course, they all would have been clamoring for that opportunity because what they <u>saw</u> with their eyes would have given them terrific confidence. Every one of them was much taller than that small adversary would have been.

This is a perfect example of "walking by sight," which is exactly the opposite of what God has told us to do. "For we walk by **faith**, not by sight" (2 Cor. 5:7). Too much of the time, our natural senses control our thinking and our decision making. We should heed God's admonition to look up higher to eternal things rather than earthly temporal things. In 2 Corinthians 4:18, God says, "While we look **not** at the things which are seen (Goliath), but at the things which are not seen (God): for the things which are seen are temporal; but the things which are not seen are eternal."

David was a man after God's own heart. He had learned from experience that God was bigger and stronger than any dilemma his natural senses perceived. A bear was stronger than David, yet by the power of God, David killed the bear. A lion was stronger than David, yet by God's power, he killed the lion also. David had learned to look above what his eyes saw and instead, focus on the Lord, who is stronger than any enemy and far above any challenge we could ever have.

When he saw Goliath with his natural eyes, he looked above him and saw the God who was FAR stronger than any giant. His focus was on God's ability, not his own. That is where we must train ourselves to look…namely, above any and every problem we may ever face. We must look to the God who always has the answer instead of looking at ourselves in relation to the problem and feeling quite overpowered by it. It just depends on where you are looking. Always look OVER Goliath's head!

God's Instrument

As I was praying this morning, I told the Lord how I wanted to be His 0.12 mm toothed forceps. I know that means nothing at all to most people, but it means a great deal to me. I wrote a book called, *An Instrument in God's Hand*, and I put copies of this book in every examination room in my office. One day, a patient who had been reading that book asked me how I could love an instrument, which was a comment I had made in my book. Let me tell you why I said that and what it means to me.

Since the first day I performed eye surgery, I have always used this forceps. I can't imagine doing surgery without it being on my tray of surgical instruments. Even if I didn't need it on a certain case, I always wanted it there just in case something arose during surgery where nothing else would meet my need like that 0.12 mm forceps. It was always there. It was clean, sterile, and laying there with no will of its own.

It was there solely to be available to me to meet my needs. That instrument had no agenda; it had no pride, and it was not upset whether I used it or not. The only purpose for its existence was to be used by me, whenever and however I chose. Over a span of forty-plus years, it has always been there, always ready to meet my need and my desire. Without me needing it and using it, it would have no purpose to exist in this world. Of course I love that instrument. What else in my life has been with me over forty years, existing only to be available when and if I needed it. It has flown across oceans with me to do surgery in foreign lands because I needed it to be available.

When anyone, anywhere saw that forceps on a TV screen as I was doing surgery on closed circuit TV, they knew that instrument was an extension of my hand. No praise was given to the instrument by those observing the surgery. All the thanks came to the surgeon. But in the heart of the surgeon, there was gratefulness for having that instrument always there, ready and willing to be nothing to anyone but the surgeon.

I hope, as you read all the words above, that you saw the application of a person being an instrument in God's hand. I want to be an instrument like that, one that God can use whenever and however He chooses. Reread what I have said about my instrument, and see if you long to be an instrument in His hand exactly like that 0.12 mm toothed forceps has been in my hand and in my heart.

I'm happy just knowing that I belong to Him.

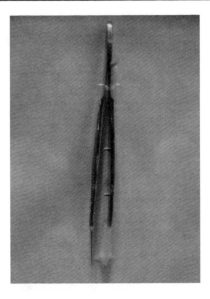

*0.12 mm toothed forceps sent to
Kathryn Kuhlman as a Christmas gift
at the instruction of the Lord. God
said she was in His hand like this
instrument had been in mine.*

Walking on the Water

Matthew 14:22-33 tells about a time when Jesus stayed on a mountain to pray while sending the disciples ahead of him in a boat on the Sea of Galilee. He prayed until sometime between three and six a.m., at which time, he proceeded to walk to the boat on the water. Of course, when the disciples saw a figure coming toward them walking on the water, they were terrified. Jesus called to them not to be afraid because it was Him. Even though the winds were blowing fiercely and the waves were high and dangerous, impetuous Peter called out to Jesus, "Lord, if it is you, command me to come to you on the water" (v. 28 AMP).

Jesus said, "Come!" So Peter got out of the boat and started walking on the water to Jesus, which was obviously a supernatural feat. As long as his eyes were fixed on Jesus, he was walking successfully, but when his focus shifted to the waves beating on his body and the wind howling in his face, he became afraid and began to sink. That is what most of us would have done on the first step if we had been brave enough to get out of the boat in the first place. So we can't throw stones at Peter for his failure. Of course, he cried out to the Lord, who reached out and saved his life. Jesus then said, "O you of little faith, why did you doubt?" (v. 31 AMP).

You may have heard sermons or even preached sermons about everything we have mentioned so far, but here is something interesting to consider. Which was easier for Peter, walking <u>away</u> from the boat or walking back <u>toward</u> the boat, and why? Did he have the same great fear walking on the water <u>to</u> the boat that he had walking <u>away</u> from it? The waves were crashing, and the wind was boisterous in both directions, for the Bible says that the wind didn't cease until they got <u>into</u> the boat (v. 32 AMP). God's word does not give us a direct answer to these questions. However, it never mentions Peter sinking anymore or crying out to Jesus anymore on the way back to the boat. It does say that Jesus "caught and held him" (v. 31 AMP).

The lesson learned is that when Jesus is holding you, there is no more fear, no more doubt, only peace, despite the storm of life you may be going through. When Peter was walking alone, he was relying on his own faith, which was too frail to withstand the storm. When he was walking with Jesus, he was relying on Jesus' faith, which is impossible to sink. He was now calm and relaxed. He wouldn't have cared if there were crocodiles or snakes in the water because Jesus was there to take care of them. To walk through our storms, we must latch onto Jesus, cling to Him, rely on Him, and never let ourselves pull away from Him, not even one millimeter. We must rely on His fathomless faith and power, not our own.

Paul takes this one step further and makes a profound statement in Galatians 2:20. "I am crucified with Christ: nevertheless I live; yet not I, but <u>Christ liveth in me</u>: and the life which I now live in the flesh I live by the <u>faith of</u> the Son of God, who loved me, and gave himself for me."

This states that it was no longer his life or his faith, but Christ's life and Christ's faith that was working through him. Our goal should be to crucify our flesh (our own will) as Paul did, and allow Jesus to live His life in and through us. Then we would no longer have to wonder if we have enough faith, for it would be His faith flowing through us, not ours.

In Ephesians 5:31, God reveals a mystery to us, namely that the "two shall become one flesh." He is speaking of Christ and His church. See this clearly: You are the flesh (body), and you are meant to be an abode for Christ to live in. He wants to be the King of the Kingdom of God within you. He wants to be the Decision Maker, the One in charge. And He wants to carry out His desires through you. "For it is God which worketh in you both to will and to do of his good pleasure" (Phil. 2:13). **Jesus needs a body.** Will you volunteer?

Sickness Unlawful

In Matthew 16:19 (NASB), Jesus tells His disciples, "I will give you the keys of the kingdom of heaven; and whatever you shall bind on earth shall have been bound in heaven, and whatever you shall loose on earth shall have been loosed in heaven." Other versions elaborate on the word "bind" by using words like refuse, forbid, lock, and declare to be improper and unlawful. I seized upon the word "**unlawful**," used in the Amplified version, as particularly powerful.

When a person is "saved" or "born again," he makes Jesus Christ his Savior and the Lord or King of his life. King Jesus sets up the kingdom of God within us (Luke 17:21). Our bodies become the temple of the Holy Ghost (1 Cor. 6:19). As in every kingdom, there are laws and privileges. One of our privileges, as children of God, is that Jesus bore our sickness, carried away our pain, and healed us (Isa. 53:4-5; 1 Peter 2:24; Matt. 8:17).

We know for a certainty that Jesus has made provision for our healing as children of God. Isaiah 53:5 states, "But he was wounded for our transgressions, he was bruised for our iniquities: the chastisement of our peace was upon him; and <u>with his stripes we are healed</u>."

It seems easy enough for people to understand and accept that His wounds, His bruises, and His shed blood on Calvary was more than enough to wash away our sins and therefore, provide salvation for us. In the very same sentence God declares that His stripes were more than enough to provide our healing, and we don't have to be sick or remain sick. How can we accept the first half of God's sentence and ignore the second half? It is time to accept both halves and receive them into our lives. We don't have to remain sick any more than we have to remain sinful. Jesus made provision for both at the same time.

Since Jesus has made provision for our healing, then it should be **unlawful** for the enemy to put sickness on us. But Satan's desire is to steal, kill and destroy everyone and everything that he can (John 10:10). God says, "Be sober, be vigilant; because your adversary the devil, as a roaring lion, walketh about, seeking whom he <u>may</u> devour" (1 Peter 5:8).

The word "may" has a permissive sense, meaning that he can't devour you unless you allow it. Many Christians simply accept a diagnosis or a symptom and do nothing about it from a spiritual standpoint. If no action is taken in the Spirit to deny the entrance of that disease or symptom, then Satan will come in and advance his plans to steal, kill, and destroy. You have given him permission to devour simply by doing nothing in the Spirit—not binding it away and declaring it **unlawful**.

Each of us is the policeman of our own body, which is the temple of the Holy Spirit (1 Cor. 6:19). For sure, the Spirit doesn't want sickness in His temple, and neither do we. So it is time that we rise up, and tell Satan and his imps from hell to vacate our property (our body) because it is **unlawful** for him to be there. We have been bought with a very high price, namely the blood of Jesus, and we belong to Him. Therefore, Satan is trespassing on God's property when he tries to come against us with sickness or any other attack from hell. As the policeman of our bodies and our being, it is up to each one of us to enforce God's word in our lives.

"Behold, I give unto you power to tread on serpents and scorpions, and over <u>all</u> the power of the enemy (Satan): and <u>nothing</u> shall by any means hurt you" (Luke 10:19).

"Submit yourselves therefore to God. <u>Resist</u> the devil, and he will flee from you" (James 4:7).

If a venomous snake came knocking at your door with the intent and ability to harm you or even kill you, you certainly would never open the door and say, "Come on in Mr. Snake." You would shut the door tightly and demand that he leave your property immediately. In fact, you would probably kill him for even being there. In the same way, if pain or vomiting or any other symptom came knocking at your door, you have the power and obligation to refuse it and demand that it leave your body in the name of Jesus. It is **unlawfully** trespassing on God's property. Jesus has done everything necessary for our health by taking those excruciating stripes on His body at Calvary. Now, it is up to us to enforce His victory over our own lives. Run over the devil before he has a chance to run over you!

Chapter 4

Healing Miracles

Seeing Without an Eye

I am going to share with you a miracle that would be hard for me to believe except for two things: 1) I know without a doubt that NOTHING is impossible with God. 2) This is a miracle concerning an eye, or actually the lack of one, which I am imminently qualified to speak about, being an eye surgeon and having examined this eye personally.

I first met Ronald Coyne when he was invited to the church I attended. He had lost his right eye from a serious eye injury when he was a child. The eye had been removed and a prosthesis placed in the empty eye socket. At some time after that, his mother took him to a meeting where a lady evangelist was praying for people to be healed. Ronald had a cold that day, so his mother told him to go down to the altar, and let this lady pray for his cold. When he got there, the evangelist took one look at his eyes and noticed the right one was not quite straight. Without asking the child why he had come for prayer, she assumed the reason was to correct the slightly deviated eye. She prayed that God would heal his eye problems, and Ronald went back to his seat.

Later in that meeting, Ronald noticed that he could now see out of his right eye socket that had no eye in it. He tugged on his mother and said, "Mother I can see."

She said, "Yes, Ronald, I know you can see. Now be quiet. The service is going on."

He obeyed her for a while, and then told her again. Finally, she realized that he was talking about seeing where there was no right eye. That was the beginning of a life testifying and demonstrating this phenomenal miracle of God.

The day he came to our church, he folded a handkerchief over several times and placed it over his good left eye. He then taped all the edges of the handkerchief so there would be no chance of seeing around it. Anyone in the congregation could bring their driver's license, a credit card, or anything else to him, and he could read all the numbers and letters perfectly through an empty eye socket with or without the prosthesis in it.

The pastor, knowing that I was an eye surgeon, called on me to examine this right eye socket and the bandage over the good left eye. I guess the Lord wanted to use me to corroborate the amazing miracle He had done. I examined his empty right orbit and the plastic prosthesis he usually wore for cosmetic reasons. I took more adhesive tape and put more over the already well covered left eye. I was <u>positive</u> he could not see around the bandage I had put over his good eye. More reading material was brought to him randomly from people in the church who had never laid eyes on Ronald before in their lives. Ronald Coyne could absolutely see without an eye!

Many say, "But that is impossible." Yes, I know. However, I also know that God gets glory from doing the impossible because NO man can take credit for doing it. Lazarus had two eyes that were dead and even rotting after four days in the grave, yet God made him see. Was it any harder for God to make Ronald Coyne see out of one missing eye than it was for Him to make Lazarus see from two dead eyes, walk with two dead and rotting legs or talk with a dead and rotting mouth? Is anything too difficult for the Lord? After all, compared to creating the whole universe, making someone see without an eye would seem like a breeze.

I would later appear on the Phil Donahue television program, giving testimony of this amazing miracle done by our great God of the impossible. Phil Donahue had invited another ophthalmologist to give his opinion of Ronald Coyne's ability to see without an eye. This doctor had never seen Ronald, never examined Ronald, and never seen this miracle demonstrated in an undeniable way. He said that he was a magician, and this trick was well known among magicians. The person would cover one eye, leaving a small space uncovered, but imperceptible to the audience. He would then read through the small space he had not covered. That was the deceptive "magical" trick. If he had been able to personally put as much tape as I put over Ronald's good eye, and been absolutely positive that there were no spaces to see through, he would have been forced into conceding that this was no magic trick, but an authentic miracle of God that defied explanation in any other way.

Isn't it interesting how people want to deny that God can and will do the impossible, so they try to figure out natural explanations for the supernatural? If they would read God's word and believe what He says in it, they would realize that the Bible is replete with examples of the supernatural—Israel crossing the Red Sea on dry ground and then the entire Egyptian army drowning as they followed God's people; Jesus walking on water or turning water into wine; Bartimaeus, who was blind, now seeing at the word of Jesus. "And Jesus said unto him, Go thy way; thy faith hath made thee whole. And immediately he received his sight…" (Mark 10:52).

We don't know if Bartimaeus had eyes or not; we just know he could see after Jesus spoke to him. Perhaps he could see without eyes like Ronald Coyne did. We cannot put the Creator of the Universe in a box, and say, "We won't believe You are able to do a thing unless we can attach natural understanding to it."

I, for one, will not put any limit whatsoever on God. He made everything that ever was or ever will be—sun, stars, moon, world, and everything in it. Of course, Ronald can see without an eye if God wills it. "Then came the word of the LORD unto Jeremiah, saying, Behold, **I *am* the LORD, the God of all flesh: is there any thing too hard for me?**" (Jeremiah 32:26-27)

Creation of a New Lung

Another spectacular miracle happened to a man that we came to know as a friend, Gene Mullinax. In 1958, as a young man in his twenties with a wife and two children, he developed a large growth in his lung, which resulted in serious bleeding with the slightest exertion. Because of this, he was unable to work, lost an excessive amount of weight, and became bedfast. The only possible solution was to surgically remove the growth, which made it necessary to also remove his entire right lung and three ribs. A large drainage hole was left in his back. After the surgery, they didn't know if he would live or die. He did survive. However, the extensive surgery left him severely incapacitated and unable to work or support his family. He spent most of the first six months after surgery in bed.

On one of the rare occasions that he left his home, he passed the Arkansas State Fairgrounds, where there was a huge tent with a sign that read, "The blind see! The deaf hear! The lame walk! Signs, Wonders, Miracles." He certainly did not believe in such things, so he drove on by, but he continued to think about it. Would God really heal people as the sign stated? He did not have faith for healing; however, he had a desperate need.

He investigated the evangelist, A.A. Allen, and even spoke with him. He explained his terrible situation to him and said he wanted to be totally healed of everything. Gene asked Reverend Allen if he thought God would heal him. The evangelist responded as though this would be nothing difficult at all for God.

Finally, Gene decided to go to the tent and expose what he considered to be false claims. When he went in, there was a line of people that needed to be healed. He got in the line, and in front of him was a man with a baby over his shoulder. Gene could see that the baby had a large tumor protruding from its mouth that obviously needed to be healed. He thought to himself that if God was able to take away that baby's tumor, then he would believe that healing from God was real. After all, a baby could not fake a healing! He watched that baby intently from close range as the line progressed toward the evangelist. Finally, it was the baby's turn, and much to Gene's astonishment, the tumor instantly disappeared in front of his eyes. Reverend Allen did not even touch the baby; he simply prayed in the name of Jesus, and the tumor left.

Gene's faith suddenly soared. "If God would heal this baby in such a miraculous way, maybe He would heal me too," Gene thought. When he stepped in front of Reverend Allen, the evangelist asked the whole congregation to join him in prayer for Gene. He asked Gene to raise his hands toward heaven, and as he did, Allen shouted, "Oh God!" Instantly Gene felt like warm oil was being poured over him. Air rushed into his chest like a balloon was being blown up. His slumped shoulder was lifted. His sunken chest was filled out, and he could breathe normally. The draining hole in his back caused by surgery was closed, and he immediately felt normal for the first time in many months. God had healed him completely!

Gene returned to the doctor who had done the surgery. He took serial x-rays over a period of months to document this phenomenal miracle. Much to everyone's amazement, the x-rays showed that his resected right lung was now replaced by a normal lung, and the three ribs that had been surgically removed were now there. Obviously, medical science had no explanation for this. Man could not do this. It had to be a miracle wrought by God.

Gene could now return to a normal life as a young man with a body full of strength and vigor. His heart was now completely different because he had had an encounter with the living, healing Jesus. He and his wife were both baptized with the Holy Ghost shortly after his healing. Gene built a very successful business, which stretched over several states. He subsequently sold his business to serve the Lord full time as pastor of a growing church in Little Rock, Arkansas.

I will stand shoulder to shoulder with Gene Mullinax and a long line of other Christians in openly declaring, "We serve a God of miracles!"

The Grief to Gazelle Miracle

In an unusual way, God has chosen to combine my strong scientific background as a medical doctor and eye surgeon with being a witness to His miraculous feats over many years. The following is an astounding medical miracle that I personally witnessed on a hot summer day in Cincinnati, Ohio, in 1993. For me, it was a very special day because it was my birthday.

I was praying for sick people at the altar of a local church, where I had been holding a revival, when a lady approached me and asked if I would come toward the back of the auditorium and pray for her sister who, she said, was unable to come to the front for prayer. Without hesitating and without thinking, I followed her. She led me halfway back through the auditorium to an aisle seat where her sister was sitting, a walker by her side.

I said to her, "Rise, in the name of Jesus, and be healed." I had no idea what her problem was. That never entered my mind. I simply took her by the arm, lifted her to her feet, and the two of us began walking down the center aisle of the church together. I say "walking," but the truth is that she was laboriously shuffling along, taking tiny baby steps. I noticed that the arm I was holding was as stiff as a board. In fact, her entire body seemed stiff and immobile. None of these facts deterred me from encouraging her to walk.

Then suddenly, a miraculous thing happened. The arm I was holding made a popping sound, and so did other parts of her body. I felt the arm become more flexible. This must have simultaneously happened in her legs because she began taking better steps. By this time, we had arrived at the altar, and I proceeded to walk with her across the front of the church building—once, then twice—and each time, she was able to walk faster, until her shuffle became actual steps. The third time we crossed the front of the altar area, we were jogging together, and I realized that she was going faster than I was!

I let go of her arm, and she took off running with all her might. She ran down the side aisle to the back of the church and then across the back. She was running like an Olympic sprinter. She came down the center aisle like she was doing the hundred yard dash in double time. I had never seen anyone run so fast in my life! She was running so fast that when she got to the altar area, there was no way she could make the turn. She didn't seem to care. Just where the center aisle ended, she slid under the communion table in the center of the altar area like a baseball player sliding into home plate and laid there under the power of God. All of us who had witnessed the event stood there in shock. A woman who had been as stiff as a board had suddenly turned into a gazelle as she was healed by the power of God.

After the service, the pastor told me the woman's story.

He and his family had gone to a local restaurant and had just ordered their food when they looked out the window and saw this lady struggling to get out of a car. She worked her feet out first, and then grimacing with pain, she very slowly hoisted herself up onto her walker. Her feet moved only in tiny steps, and each tiny step seemed to take great effort and cause her excruciating pain.

The pastor's food arrived, the family had finished eating and were already gathering their belongings and preparing to leave the restaurant by the time the lady and her sister who accompanied her were able to make it through the front door and to a table nearby. It had taken her more than thirty minutes to get inside and get seated.

Feeling great compassion for the woman and recognizing that she desperately needed a miracle, the pastor spoke with her and her sister and told them about our revival meetings the following week. God would be doing miracles, he told them, and he hoped that they would attend. The lady answered that her doctors had done everything they knew to do, but were unable to help her further with her crippling disease. It was only after the pastor had encouraged them further that they had promised that they would try to come. Thankfully, they came, for God turned her severe pain and grief into gazelle-like mobility and speed…nothing short of an astounding miracle! Thank you Jesus!

The Resurrection Miracle

In our years of owning a television station, we met a number of people with fabulous experiences with the power of Jesus. Gertrude Ticer was such a person. She had severe multiple sclerosis, which made her bedfast and struggling for life on numerous occasions. The ambulance would be called to rush her to the hospital, and time after time, she would tell the ambulance driver, "Don't forget my shoes."

They thought she was a little crazy for making such a request since she couldn't even move off of the bed, much less walk. They would say, "Gertrude, you have no need for those shoes." But she would always insist that she have them with her because she said that Jesus was going to heal her, and she would need her shoes to walk out of the hospital. They would adhere to her wishes and bring the shoes, even though they thought it was a ridiculous request.

The doctors told her that she would become blind and totally paralyzed, and this did come to pass. As she got worse and worse, they rushed her to the hospital once again. In the hospital, she had three heart attacks and one stroke. When they put her under an oxygen tent to sustain life, she said to herself that there was room for two under there, Jesus and her. She knew death was eminent.

The Lord had been calling her to preach for Him. She told Him that she couldn't do it because she didn't speak English well. He said to go anyway. Then she said she didn't know the Bible well enough. He said He would teach her. She said she was a woman. He said He knew that, and that didn't matter. Gertrude knew that if she didn't yield to the call of God, she would die very soon.

One day, a lady named Beatrice walked into her room and asked if she believed that God could heal her and asked if she wanted prayer. She said, "Yes," so the lady prayed and left the room. The Lord then spoke to Gertrude in an audible voice, and said, "I sent this woman to you." Immediately, Gertrude called for the lady to come back and told her what God had said.

Beatrice then explained that God had spoken to her in Maryland, telling her to go to Las Vegas and pray for people in incurable wards. She had taken a bus there and immediately started going from hospital to hospital praying for people. The Lord instructed her to ask them the same two questions she had asked Gertrude, "Do you believe God can heal you, and do you want prayer?" He said that one day a woman would respond saying, "God sent you to me." And that would be the person she was sent there to pray diligently for.

Beatrice began fasting and praying on that hot day in July with no food or water. Every day she would come to the hospital, and every day Gertrude got worse. On the third day, Gertrude's family was called and told to make funeral arrangements because she could die at any time.

When Beatrice came that day, she said to Gertrude, "If you were very thirsty, and you drank the glass of water on your night stand, your thirst would be quenched. On the other hand, if you looked at the glass full of water, and you knew for sure that it would quench your thirst, but you did not drink it, your thirst would remain. That is the way you are. You believe that God will heal you, but you haven't <u>received</u> the healing into yourself in a definite way. You need to <u>receive</u> it by faith the same way that you received Jesus as your Savior."

"What things soever ye desire, when ye pray, **BELIEVE** that ye **RECEIVE** them, and ye shall have them" (Mark 11:24).

As I recall the story the way Gertrude told it to us, the nurse had pulled the sheet over her face and signed the death papers on her. In her heart, she was still telling the Lord that she was afraid she would not be able to do what He wanted her to do if she were healed. Jesus told her to simply go and tell how He healed her. She felt she could do that, so she said, "Yes, Lord. I will go." She took the cup of healing and drank it, <u>receiving</u> it into herself.

At that point, Jesus walked into the room and touched her body with the tips of His fingers. It felt like fire going through her entire body. Her total blindness left, and she could see Jesus. Her bones began to crack as they straightened out, for she had been severely deformed with her muscles like cement and her limbs twisted and drawn up.

The resurrection power of Jesus Christ flooded through her body, and she became completely whole. She jumped over the bed rail, put on her shoes (the ones she always demanded that they bring to the hospital), and she walked out of the room and down the hall. Two of the nurses saw her and fainted. They had to be carried out on stretchers. The head nurse told her that she couldn't be walking down the hall because she couldn't walk and that she couldn't be alive because she had already signed her death papers. Everyone was in shock. Other patients fell on their knees when they saw her and began to pray, realizing that God had performed an undeniable miracle.

When the hospital staff came the next morning to treat her severe bedsore, they found that the affected area was now perfect. They exclaimed that this was a true miracle because the bedsore had destroyed the flesh down to the exposed bone, and there was no way this could become perfect overnight.

Jesus also made a sign and a wonder out of her bed; it would give people a shock as they touched it. He had instructed her to stay in the hospital for three days and three nights, during which time Jesus healed other patients as Gertrude prayed for them.

The entire city of Las Vegas was in a stir over what the Lord had done. People who didn't believe in God or Jesus were convinced by this miracle that Jesus truly is real and alive in this world today. Throughout Gertrude's life, many others were healed by her prayers, and many souls came into the kingdom of God through her testimony, perpetuating the power of this resurrection miracle.

God had been merciful to Gertrude and sent Beatrice to help her see how to receive. But let's look at this from God's perspective, and see if she could have received her healing much earlier. Let's go back to what Gertrude would always tell the ambulance drivers. "Jesus is <u>going to</u> heal me."

You might look at that statement and say it is correct, however, look at the tense. She was speaking of some <u>future</u> event. Every time she thought it or said it, it was still in the future, which would never accomplish her desire to be healed in the <u>present</u>. Our healing is not a future event, Jesus has already healed us. Our healing is a <u>past</u> event, "by whose stripes ye <u>were</u> healed" (1 Peter 2:24).

God said it was finished. Therefore, it is finished.

Everything that needed to be done about our healing has already been done by Jesus on that whipping post at His crucifixion. Now, we walk by faith and not by sight. In other words, we believe what God says more than we believe what our bodies say or what the doctors say or what the lab tests show. Those things are all facts in the natural. But we walk in the Spirit, meaning we walk in the truth of God's word, which supersedes and actually controls the natural. "While we look not at the things which are seen, but at the things which are not seen: for the things which are seen are temporal; but the things which are not seen are eternal" (2 Cor. 4:18).

God says that He "calleth those things which be not as though they were" (Rom. 4:17). He also says, "Thou shalt also decree a thing, and it shall be established unto thee" (Job 22:28). What would have been ideal is for Gertrude to have believed in her heart and decreed with her mouth, "I **am** healed by the stripes of Jesus." In God's eyes, that would have been correct. He also says, "What things soever ye desire, <u>when ye pray</u>, believe that ye receive them, and ye shall have them" (Mark 11:24). So the time we are to receive our requests is when we pray, not sometime in the unknown future. Whether we see the answer immediately or not is irrelevant. We receive it from God's hand the moment we pray and cling to the truth of His word.

This is certainly no indictment on Gertrude, for we all have to learn this lesson. Some learn it the hard way, and some never learn it at all. But God has made His word clear to us today, so it is up to us to walk in it from this moment forward. Amen.

Gertrude Ticer

Chapter 5

Dreams and Visions

The Unique Room

In March of 1994, I was invited by the Chinese Academy of Medical Sciences to go to Beijing and lecture on modern eye surgery. I wondered if they would want me to perform surgery. This brought up another important question. Should I take my own instruments in case the hospital where I would be teaching didn't have the instruments I needed? I was hesitant to take them since my instruments for microsurgery are very delicate and expensive. If an instrument was not handled with care, it could be damaged and cost me several thousand dollars to replace.

Two friends would be accompanying me, Geri and Susan, both veterans of the mission field. I wanted to teach one of them how to care for my instruments. Susan would have been the most likely candidate to learn, but she lived in Virginia, which was too far away. Geri was the kind of person who had a very real aversion to all things medical. If something surgical came on the television, she would leave the room. She did not want to hear about surgery, much less see it.

Would I dare ask her to learn about my surgical instruments? Because of her proximity, Geri was the only logical choice, so I asked her if she would be willing to learn how to care for my instruments. Much to my surprise, she immediately said she would. I could not imagine why she had so quickly and easily agreed to be involved with surgery, which she so obviously and vigorously disliked.

Then she shared a dream with me that God had given her several months before. In the dream, she was pushing my surgical instruments on a very old cart in a room, which she remembered vividly. The room was hexagonal in shape and had dark wood paneling with hallways going out of it in several directions. She noted foreign faces on the medical personnel, but she did not know what country she was in. This dream had made such an impression on Geri that she readily agreed to learn about the care of my surgical instruments. It is interesting how a word or a dream from God can completely change one's thinking. Geri learned a little about my instruments, and off we went with them to China.

The morning I was to lecture, we were picked up at the hotel and taken to a highly revered medical institution that had been built by John D. Rockefeller in 1921, on property originally owned by the Presbyterian Church. It was like the Harvard of China. The head of the Ophthalmology Department met us, and I began walking with him into the building. Geri and Susan followed us a few feet behind.

As we walked into the large entry room, I heard someone say, "This is it! This is it!" I turned and saw Geri with tears streaming down her face. This was the exact room God had shown her in the dream about nine months previously. It was hexagonal in shape with dark wood paneling, and it had hallways going off in various directions. How many rooms have you seen like that anywhere in the world?

Susan said blandly, "Oh, we've traveled among the nations by vision for years." But Geri's bubble was not burst. She was overwhelmed that God would show her the inside of a hospital room on the opposite side of the world and then take her to that very spot.

In the years ahead, we often told this story to the Chinese people, and many of them, who were not supposed to believe in God, would say, "Surely the God has sent you to us." They believed, as did we, that giving one a dream and then making it a reality in every detail was a miracle from God.

Dr. Vaughan teaching modern eye
surgery to surgeons in Beijing.

The Great Light

On one of my trips to Xian, China, I was left alone in the hotel room while my traveling companions were off seeing some of the sights. I knelt beside the bed and began to pray. As I prayed, I had a vision of a Chinese man sitting on the floor with his arms around his bent legs and his head down on his knees. He was in total darkness and hopelessness. He was blind, so his world was black, and he had no hope whatsoever that his situation would ever change. All the days of his life, he was sure he would sit in blackness until the day he died.

I had never felt hopelessness before, but I felt this man's hopelessness. It was a feeling too horrible to describe. I began to weep for him as I felt what he was feeling. Then suddenly the Word of the Lord came like a bolt of lightning into the pitch-black darkness!

"The people which sat in darkness saw great light" (Matt. 4:16).

My tears turned to rejoicing, and I knew in an instant that God would bring both physical and spiritual light to these people who were sitting in darkness. He would make a way for us to treat the eye diseases (cataracts, glaucoma, etc.) of the people in rural China, many of whom were very poor and had no eye care at all. And He would make a way for the light of the Gospel of Jesus Christ to be shed abroad in their hearts.

Isaiah had prophesied of Jesus, the Great Light, seven hundred years before the birth of Christ. "The people that walked in darkness have seen a great light: they that dwell in the land of the shadow of death, upon them hath the light shined" (Isa. 9:2).

Now, nearly two thousand years after Christ first shined His light among men, He was still shining it brightly into dark hearts. He had not changed.

"Jesus Christ the same yesterday, and today, and forever" (Heb. 13:8).

Advice from the Enemy

Geri had a curious dream one night. Two water snakes were swimming slowly toward us. They were swimming in parallel and appeared oriental. We were standing on the shore watching them as they swam closer and closer. When they got to the shoreline, they each slowly turned outward and swam back in the direction from which they had come, still swimming parallel to each other. We had no idea what this dream meant, but soon we were to discover that it was a warning from God.

A few days after this dream, two oriental men came to us with their opinion about the direction of the ministry God had put in our hands. Actually, it was a poor attempt from Satan because what they said was opposite from what God had already shown us. So their words had no chance whatsoever of succeeding. But we were glad that the Lord had warned us before they came, to be doubly sure that we would not be influenced by their advice.

The Window with No Pane

I had a dream in which I was going around to the windows in my house and checking them to be sure that they were all closed and locked securely. They were all closed, but I had to lock a few that were not locked. Then I came to one window that was wide open. I tried to pull it down to shut it, but noticed that there was no pane in the window. Of course there was no way to secure the whole house with one window wide open. I was very alarmed by this and said we must immediately call someone to install the missing pane.

When I awoke, I pondered that dream, not knowing what the window without a pane represented. I certainly wanted no breech in the security of our lives. I felt like the open window represented something in the Spirit, which of course would have repercussions in the natural. I asked God to show me what this meant, so I could rectify the problem.

One day, the Lord called me aside and said He would explain it to me. You have to understand the background of our lives to understand what He showed me. Geri had been very ill for a very long time (fifteen years at the time of this writing). She had nearly died on numerous occasions. Despite getting a wonderful kidney transplant, which saved her life, she had had recurring and progressing physical problems. These were caused by the anti-rejection medications she was taking to prevent rejection of the transplanted kidney. Side effects were common with such medications. The worst one was diabetes, which caused progressive problems in many parts of her body. We found ourselves living with a continual parade of new symptoms arriving almost daily, and dealing with them day in and day out.

We are strong Christians and believe God's word with all our hearts. We teach the word and admonish others to walk in the word. In fact, I am a

stickler about not saying things contrary to the word. This becomes difficult when called upon to explain why I have to handle so many phone calls
for Geri. (Natural answer: because she has difficulty hearing, even with
hearing aids.) Why can't she walk? (Natural answer: her legs and back are
too weak.) Why are they so weak? (Natural answer: she had back surgery,
plus she has diabetic neuropathy, which causes numbness of her feet.)

Well, I could go on and on, but you get the picture. Because of these
issues, I had become accustomed to explaining to people, "She has diabetic neuropathy," or "She can't hear very well," etc. Actually, I said as little
about it as possible and would not answer most questions unless forced
to. Usually, it was with another doctor who was trying to help Geri and
who needed to know the facts. Geri had become accustomed to giving
explanations about all kinds of physical symptoms to her friends and family members.

The Lord showed me that the window without a pane that was allowing
the enemy to ravage our lives was our words. Let me give you an example
by making two vertical columns with a minus sign at the top of the left
column and a plus sign at the top of the right column. Example:

- What Satan says	+ What God says
Walking by sight (enables demons to act)	Walking by faith (enables angels to act)
Geri can't walk	I can do all things through Christ (Phil. 4:13)
Geri has continual pain	Jesus has carried our pain (Isa. 53:4)
Geri has diabetic neuropathy	By His stripes we are healed (Isa. 53:5)

We have a choice in what we believe and what we say. We can agree with Satan by repeating the negative things we see in our lives or we can agree with God by repeating the positive things He says about us in His Word. We are well aware that "death and life are in the power of the tongue" (Prov. 18:21). We know that we will have whatever we say (Mark 11:23).

How long will it take us to tighten up the purse strings of our mouths and determine <u>never</u> again to agree with what Satan has put on us, <u>never</u> again say what he says about us or anyone else. That is simply having a window in the house of your life that has no pane in it. You are empowering the enemy to put even more grief on you through the open window. You can rebuke him and yell at him or do whatever you want to do, but the demons can still come in at will if you have an open window because of your words.

You might wonder how you can say you are healed when your body is still racked with pain or impaired in function. The answer is simple. You are made in the image of God. He calls things that be not as though they were (Rom. 4:17), and so should we. Actually, we can honestly say we are healed despite what our body or the medical reports tell us because God says we are healed by the stripes of Jesus. We can choose to walk by faith (believing and speaking God's word) or walk by sight (believing and speaking what the medical reports or even your symptoms indicate). A righteous man walks by <u>faith</u> and not by sight (2 Cor. 5:7). Walking by faith is trusting in God and His word. Walking by sight is believing what you feel, see or hear more than you believe God and His word.

Let me make something very clear. I believe in doctors and medicine and surgery. Remember, I am an eye surgeon and have seen God answer many people's prayers through surgery or medical treatment. If you go to a doctor and pay him or her to tell you what is wrong and what to do about it, then the likelihood is that you should heed their advice. Why bother going to the doctor if you are not going to do what they tell you to do? God and medicine are not at odds with each other. God uses medical science to heal. I am positive of that. My suggestion is to do as the doctor recommends (unless the Holy Spirit leads you not to), and at the same time, believe God's word, and speak it with your mouth. "With the heart man believes unto righteousness; and with the mouth confession is made unto salvation" (Rom. 10:10). This law of God applies to your health, your longevity, your finances, and every other area of your life. Believing what God says above every natural circumstance and speaking it with your mouth brings deliverance in any area.

Frankly, I am tired of Satan "eating our lunch" as Christians. We have been given power over all the power of the enemy, and nothing shall by any means harm us (Luke 10:19). However, that can only be true if we have all of our windows shut, including the window of our <u>mouths</u>. We need to ask God to forgive us for not using the sword of the Spirit, which is the word of God, to counteract every wrong thought or word that is thrown at us (Eph. 6:17).

My decision is this. I have asked the Lord to forgive me for saying negative things about my friend without realizing it. My window is shut with a strong pane in it as of this moment, and it will stay shut all the days of my life. How about you?

I recently read an article by a man who had been a satanic high priest. He is now a consecrated Christian and wants people to recognize the tactics of the enemy. This man is an authority on the subject since he worked for Satan twenty-five years. He explains that there are three "gates" through which the enemy can attack us. One is the "mouth gate," which God made very clear to me through the dream of the window with no pane. Two other "gates" are the "eye gate" and the "ear gate." To guard ourselves against having these gates open, we must put a tight control over what we watch on TV, the Internet, in movies, etc. We must eliminate wrong books, magazines, and every other potential source of filth.

It seems like everywhere you turn in this world, darts of violence, sex, bad language, and wrong thoughts are being hurled at you, even through some commercials. With the help of the Holy Spirit, we can recognize and barricade these wrong gates and live a clean life without temptations from hell. In fact, this expert on Satan says that one of the best ways to stop the devil in his tracks is to have a <u>godly character</u>. That is attainable and should be a priority in our lives. Let's shut all the open windows and gates in our lives and walk free and happy in Jesus.

Scorpions Everywhere

Geri once had a dream where she was landing in some vehicle similar to a helicopter. As she looked out of the vehicle, there were scorpions on every square inch of the land. The amazing thing was that when she put her foot on the ground, the scorpions scattered. With every step she took, the scorpions ran away before the sole of her foot hit the ground.

When Jesus sent out seventy disciples, two by two, they came back saying, "Lord, even the devils are subject unto us through thy name." The Lord's response was, "I beheld Satan as lightning fall from heaven. Behold, I give unto you power to tread on serpents and <u>scorpions</u>, and over all the power of the enemy: and nothing shall by any means hurt you" (Luke 10:17-19). We understand that when Jesus said "serpents and scorpions," He was referring to demons and devils and all the forces of hell. He very clearly said that He has given us power and dominion over all of these evil forces.

Geri's dream was a beautiful demonstration of the words of Jesus. It left no doubt that the scorpions (demons) were scared to death of her—and of all of us who know who we are in Christ Jesus. They are under our feet!

The Snake

While on a trip to the east coast, Geri had a very vivid dream of a snake. It was coiled and ready to strike at her head. In her dream, she quickly put her hands up to protect her face. The snake struck both hands, but the right one was wounded more than the left one. The snake attached itself to her right hand. She shook it off, and when it hit the ground, it turned to ashes.

When she awoke, she was visibly shaken. She had been petrified of snakes all of her life. In fact, years before the dream, we were flying over Pakistan at night. Geri was looking out the window into total darkness. She turned to me and asked, "If this plane crashed right now, do you think there would be cobras on the ground?" I told her that if the plane crashed, she wouldn't have to be worried about cobras.

Soon after the dream, she began having severe pain in her hands, especially her right hand. Keep in mind that Geri was an anointed organist, so her hands were crucial to the flow of her anointing. She tried over the counter medications, but the pain was too severe to be helped by those drugs. Finally, she went to the doctor who gave her prescription medication to help control the inflammation and pain. This medication helped somewhat, but she still lived in pain. The last two fingers of her right hand ended up with permanent crippling contractures.

As we matured in God, we realized that the dream had been a warning from God of an impending attack of the enemy. If we had realized that at the time she had the dream, we would have taken authority over it, and declared it null and void in the name of Jesus. God's word says, "My people are destroyed for lack of knowledge" (Hos. 4:6). We were young in God and definitely lacked knowledge at the time Geri had the dream, and she suffered the consequences of our ignorance. God clearly says, "Verily I say unto you, whatsoever ye shall bind (lock, forbid) on earth shall be bound in heaven: and whatsoever ye shall loose (unlock, permit) on earth shall be loosed in heaven" (Matt. 18:18). We could have easily bound the dream away from becoming manifest at the time Geri had the dream. Then she would never have suffered the pain and repercussions of the devil's attack. His efforts would have been thwarted completely.

Another instance of being warned in advance of an impending attack comes from the life of my good friend, Ruth Ward Heflin. The Lord had told her to make a trip by train across China and Russia. At every stop she was to pray for the land and the people. She would set an alarm if the stops were scheduled at night, so she would not miss praying.

When she was in Australia, someone had a vision of something happening to her on the next to the last stop on her journey across Russia. She chose to think positively and "look forward to the good thing that would happen to me at that stop." Thinking positively won't thwart the plans of the devil. They have to be cancelled by applying the word of God in the power of the name of Jesus. Ruth fell on ice as she was getting off of the train at that very stop and broke her ankle. This caused her untold grief as she continued her travels across Russia and for years to come after that.

I am relating these events to you in hopes that you will learn from our mistakes, and NEVER allow the enemy to put bad things on you, whether warned in advance or not. "Be sober, be vigilant; because your adversary the devil, as a roaring lion, walketh about, seeking whom he <u>may</u> devour" (1 Peter 5:8). Notice the word "may." May has a permissive sense, meaning you have to <u>permit</u> him to devour you. If you do nothing in the Spirit, then he has freedom to destroy you without any resistance. Of course, that is what he does to many people unfortunately, including ignorant Christians.

Note: In relating these dreams to you, I noticed that several of them were given forewarnings of some impending negative event. If we are wise, then we should see red flags and take immediate action when God gives us a dream or vision as a warning.

The River

One night, God gave me a dream that impacted the rest of my life. I was standing on a high ledge, about fifteen feet high, overlooking a river. There was a man near me that was pacing back and forth, obviously in great anxiety and despair. He had a wife and daughter who were looking on. As I watched this man, I began telling him he needed to jump in the river. He brushed aside my comment and continued to pace. I said it to him again more forcefully, and again, he did not respond. Finally, I became very emphatic, telling him he must jump. This time, he said, "OK." It seemed like he complied just to get me to stop insisting. The four of us all jumped into the river together—the man, his wife, his daughter, and me.

Once in the water, every care left this man. He became so relaxed and carefree, as if the overwhelming burdens of a few minutes ago never existed. He was smiling and floating. He seemed so very happy and at perfect ease. I understood why because I felt that way also. The water had a buoyancy to it, and there was no need to exert any effort whatsoever. The river itself held you up. Every muscle in your body could totally relax. This was not an earthly feeling. An instantaneous gush of peace, joy, and relaxation overwhelmed you the moment you hit the water.

Many times, dreams elude one's understanding, but the moment I awoke, I realized this river was the one described in Ezekiel 47 as coming from the sanctuary of God. It had life in it! "Everything that touches the water of this river will live" (Ezek. 47:9 NLT). That "everything" included fish, trees, and especially us. For the first time in our lives, we were experiencing life as God had intended it to be. The water is symbolic of the Holy Spirit, and we were floating in Him. There can be nothing more glorious than to be surrounded and upheld by the Holy Spirit. I decided I never wanted to leave this river as long as I lived. I never wanted to return to fleshly thoughts and problems, but instead, I wanted to live life with the Spirit of God in control.

Reflecting on this dream, many things became clear to me. If you threw a piece of wood into a stream, it would go wherever the flow of the water took it. The course of the wood would be at the total discretion of the river. The wood would not have to worry about where it was going. The stream would decide that. It would not have to worry about keeping its head above water; the stream would handle that. In other words, the wood would be completely carefree because the decisions of its life belonged to the river.

In like manner, the Lord wants us to yield our lives to Him and let Him decide where He wants to take us and how He wants to use us. He wants us to repose in His arms. He wants our lives to belong to Him. Jesus is the example of that. He said:

"The Son can do nothing of himself, but what he seeth the Father do: for what things soever he doeth, these also doeth the Son likewise" (John 5:19).

"My meat is to do the will of him that sent me, and to finish His work" (John 4:34).

"Not my will, but thine, be done" (Luke 22:42).

He had no will of His own. He had abdicated it to the will of the Father. God was in complete control of Jesus, which resulted in Jesus saying, "Come unto me, all ye that labour and are heavy laden, and I will give you rest. Take my yoke upon you, and learn of me; for I am meek and lowly in heart: and ye shall find rest unto your souls. For my yoke is easy, and my burden is light" (Matt. 11:28-30).

He had found rest for His soul. He had found a burden in life that was easy and light. What was that yoke, that burden? To yield to the Father entirely at all times. Jesus was living in the river, and we can too. It is a life available to every single one of us who will give their lives to God to do with what He chooses. Sounds simple doesn't it? It is as simple as jumping in the river and trusting Him for everything.

Twelve O'Clock

I am going to relate to you two dreams concerning ministry that I had many years ago. In the first dream, there were people standing out of doors. I was on an elevated area leading them. We all seemed lost in worshipping God, oblivious to the time. Suddenly, people started rushing to the embankment where I was standing and falling on their knees, asking God to save them. No call for salvation had been made. They were crying out to God with all their hearts from a spontaneous motivation within themselves. In the dream, I thought this was wonderful.

Immediately after the wave of people being saved, another wave began as spontaneously as the first. This time, people were coming to "the altar," which was just a dirt embankment, and bringing money. Again, this was totally unsolicited. I looked at my watch, and the time was ten minutes until twelve o'clock. I knew we had one hour for this meeting and that the cut off time was twelve o'clock sharp. We had lost track of time in worshipping the Lord, and now we had very little time left. I tried to get them to stop bringing money because I had not yet shared the word of God with them. I thought sharing God's word was more important than bringing money in the short time remaining. No matter how vigorously I tried to get them to stop coming, they ignored my pleas and kept bringing money anyway. When my dream ended, it was five minutes until twelve.

When I awoke, it seemed to me that this was an end-time dream with a definite, fixed time limit still available to us. It was interesting that we were lost in worship for about fifty minutes of the allotted sixty minutes given to us. Of course, we have no idea what five minutes or an hour means to God. He obviously doesn't count time as we do, but I can tell you, we don't have much time left. In the dream, I felt an urgency in my spirit that we must work very quickly and that twelve o'clock would definitely be the end of the time available. That was an absolute.

"The harvest truly is great, but the labourers are few: pray ye therefore the Lord of the harvest, that he would send forth labourers into his harvest. Go your ways: behold, I send you..." (Luke 10:2-3).

In the second dream, I had come out onto a large stage with footlights. As I looked out at the people gathered there, it was a huge crowd that went farther than the eye could see. My thought at that point was that only Jesus could handle this situation. Only Jesus would know what to say and how to minister to thousands or millions all at the same time. He would know the words that would affect the heart of every person there. He would have the power to heal their broken hearts and diseased bodies. He could make the pain go away. No one else in all of God's creation could do this but Jesus.

The wonderful thing about standing on that stage by myself was knowing that Jesus was there with me. I looked like I was alone, but I really was not. The Creator of the Universe was there to do everything that needed to be done for every single person there. They had come to be fed spiritually and healed of every kind of infirmity imaginable, and Jesus knew all about each one of them. Isn't He magnificent! Isn't He wonderful beyond words! Is anything too difficult for Him?

In reflecting on this dream, I am so very thankful to know that whatever stage or open field or any other place the Lord puts me, He will always be there with me and in me. He will be the One doing the works. My part is to show up, and be nothing. His part is to be everything. **All He needs is a body!**

The Eye Surgery Dream

Before the days of LASIK surgery, there was a surgical technique called Radial Keratotomy (RK), which was done to correct nearsightedness (myopia). I had patients flooding into my practice who wanted this surgery. John, the husband of one of my employees, had myopia, but he never showed any interest in having RK surgery. For several years, his wife would talk about it, but John remained uninterested.

Much to my surprise, John came in for an examination one day and said he wanted me to do RK surgery on him. I was puzzled by this change in attitude and asked him why he had now decided to have the surgery. His answer affected my thinking for the rest of my life.

He told me that he had a dream many years before in which someone was doing eye surgery on him, and he went blind. Obviously, he had a very strong aversion to eye surgery since that dream. He then told me of a recent dream God had given him in which he was again having eye surgery. In this dream, I was doing surgery on him. He saw Jesus come from the corner of the room, put His hands over mine, and perform RK surgery. Upon awakening, he was now very enthusiastic about the surgery and could hardly wait to come and see me to have it done!

You can see why John's dream changed my thinking as well as his. I imagine it will change your thinking also, by recognizing the fact that Jesus is actively involved in treating His children, whether with medicines or surgery or outright miracles. Jesus is in the healing business. John did have the surgery with a good result and was grateful to God for the dream that guided his decision to have it.

Another patient came in during the LASIK era and wanted me to do the surgery on her to get rid of very severe myopia. She was a pastor's wife from Louisiana. We did all the necessary examinations and scheduled her for surgery. The day before surgery, she and her husband drove from Louisiana and spent the night in a motel since the surgery was to be done early the next morning. That night she became frightened of having the surgery. She was planning to call my office the next morning and cancel the surgery because of the overwhelming fear.

As she was praying about it, the Lord reminded her of her fervent prayer as a child. She hated her thick glasses and would pray over and over to God to get rid of them. That never happened, and as she grew older, she forgot about her prayer. She didn't even remember it at all until the Lord reminded her of it. Isn't it interesting that we forget what we prayed, but God never forgets our prayers? The answer may take years in coming, but we can be sure that "the effectual fervent prayer of a righteous man availeth much" (James 5:16).

After reminding her of her prayer, the Lord then said to her, "Tomorrow, I am going to answer your prayer through LASIK surgery with Dr. Vaughan." Suddenly, all of her fear melted away, and she felt confident of an excellent outcome. On the morning of surgery, she told me this story before the surgery began. God kept His word and gave her an excellent result. After all, He is **The Great Physician**.

Chapter 6

Life-Changing Revelations

The Plateau of Promise

I once heard of a modern-day shepherd who had drawn parallels between his experience with sheep and the 23rd Psalm. From him, I learned that sheep are taken to a high plateau or tableland in the summer for grazing. During the months leading up to summer, the shepherd has made many trips to this plateau to carefully prepare it for his sheep. He has pulled up many poisonous plants that could kill his sheep. He has trapped and killed as many potential predators as possible to protect his sheep. He has dug anew the water wells that may have been covered over with sticks and dirt during the long winter months. He has done everything he can to make sure this plateau is as perfect as possible for his sheep to spend the warm summer months.

In order to get there, they must go through valleys where dangers lurk. Torrential rain can cause rivers to swell to dangerous levels. Mud slides or rock slides can endanger the herd. Predators can watch the sheep from high vantage points to find the right time and the right sheep to attack. All of these real dangers bring about the wording, "Yea, though I walk through the valley of the shadow of death, I will fear no evil: for thou art with me…" (Ps. 23:4). The word "through" is a critical one, denoting that there is every expectation of coming out at the other end of the valley. The sheep draw their sense of security from the presence of the shepherd. Actually, they look to him as their sole source of defense.

When they finally get through this "valley of the shadow of death," they step out onto a plateau or tableland. Here, they have the pleasure of grazing on delicious foliage in ideal weather with plenty of cool, clean water. It was definitely worth the long journey up the valley, despite the dangers. The shepherd is closer to the sheep during the summer spent on this high plateau (or tableland) than at any other time. He has no house to go home to at night, so he sleeps with the sheep. They are his constant and only companions. His eyes are always on them. They have his undivided attention. Even though predators are always around, the shepherd has minimized their threat by his preparations, which David describes with these words: "Thou preparest a table (tableland or plateau) before me in the presence of mine enemies…" (Ps. 23:5).

Home Base:

As I was thinking about this, the Lord showed me that there are basically four places that we, His sheep, can be in His kingdom. Let's call the first place "home base." The sheep belong to the shepherd (Jesus) there. He cares for them because they are His. He has bought them with the highest price a man could pay—namely, the shed blood of Jesus at Calvary. He makes sure they have clean water, nourishing grass, and shelter from the storms. To be in this home base, a person must be "born again" or saved. He must ask God to forgive him of the sin in his life (repent), turn away from the ways offensive to God, and then accept Jesus Christ as his Lord and Savior. He then becomes one of Jesus' sheep and can live in the security of his home base. He has the assurance that when he dies he will have a home in heaven. This salvation is a free gift from God to everyone who will trust in, rely on, and cling to His Son, Jesus Christ. So let's call home base God's **first gift**, received by us when we were sinners.

Jesus would like to take us to higher ground if we will follow Him. Since we have been given a free will, we can chose to follow Him or stay at "home base" where things are familiar, and we feel comfortable. After all, who knows where we will end up if we leave this familiar spot and decide to follow Him into the unknown?

Most Christians will make the decision to stay in that spot that they know best. In fact, most don't even realize there is any other place in Christ. They know they will have a place in heaven because they have accepted Jesus as their savior, but they haven't sought after the deeper things of God with their whole hearts. I identify with living at this "home base." For many years of my life, I did not realize that there was anything else available to me. But as I began to study the Bible in a serious way on my own, I discovered there was much more in this life as a Christian that I had never experienced, and I wanted everything that Jesus would lead me into.

Base Camp:

Jesus said in Luke 24:49, "And, behold, I send the promise of my Father upon you: but tarry ye in the city of Jerusalem, until ye be endued with power from on high." What was this "promise of the Father," and what was this power that I had not known about? I discovered the answer in Acts 1:5, 8 "For John truly baptized with water; but ye shall be <u>baptized with the Holy Ghost</u> not many days hence. … But ye shall receive <u>power</u>, after that the Holy Ghost is come upon you: and ye shall be <u>witnesses</u> unto me both in Jerusalem, and in all Judaea, and in Samaria, and unto the uttermost part of the earth." So I now understood that God the Father had promised to give us His power, which He called being "baptized with the Holy Ghost," for the purpose of making us powerful witnesses of Jesus to all the world.

This definitely sounded like something I wanted and needed, but how can I receive it? Jesus gave us the simple answer to that in Luke 11:11-13. "If a son shall ask bread of any of you that is a father, will he give him a stone? or if he ask a fish, will he for a fish give him a serpent? Or if he shall ask an egg, will he offer him a scorpion? If ye then, being evil, know how to give good gifts unto your children: how much more shall your heavenly Father give the Holy Spirit to them that ask him?"

I was a child of God, so all I had to do was ask my Father for this gift of His Holy Spirit, and He promised to give it to me. I knelt in my living room alone and asked in faith, believing God's word. I thanked Him for filling me with the Holy Spirit. I got up and went about my household chores. No angels appeared, no flashing lights, no supernatural phenomenon appeared as I prayed. However, my life immediately changed. I was on fire as a witness for God like I had never been before. I was so happy in my newfound closeness to Him. I plunged into studying my Bible with newfound fervor. Life was so exciting! It became clear that this was the **second gift** from God, which was free to any child of His who asked for it.

When serious climbers are trying to tackle a mountain like Everest, they set up a base camp on the mountain at a moderately high elevation where they keep their supplies to equip them for an even higher climb. So Christians, who have left "home base" and have been baptized with the Holy Spirit by Jesus, are led to what let's call the spiritual "base camp." Life is different there. Their newfound exuberance and devotion may be manifested in a variety of ways that were not exhibited in "home base." The gifts of the Holy Spirit mentioned in 1 Corinthians 12:7-11 are in operation now. People often lift their hands while worshipping God. Some dance in the Spirit.

Like on the day of Pentecost (Acts 2:4), those baptized with the Holy Spirit can speak in tongues. This should be no surprise since Jesus said that they would. "And these signs shall follow them that believe; In my name they shall cast out devils; they shall speak with new tongues…" (Mark 16:17). Speaking in tongues has many advantages. "He that speaketh in an unknown tongue edifieth himself" (1 Cor. 14:4). "But ye, beloved, building up yourselves on your most holy faith, praying in the Holy Ghost" (Jude 1:20). I would think every Christian would like to be edified and have their faith built up as God says praying in tongues will do.

Sooner or later, people get comfortable in this setting with other like-minded Christians in the base camp. Often they feel like they have arrived at the pinnacle of what God has for them. But the truth is that Jesus is still beckoning to them to come up higher.

Valley of the Shadow of Death:

If you study God's word carefully, it is clear that there are even higher realms of God where miracles and healings are common occurrences. You realize that there are still things promised by Jesus that you don't see manifested to the fullest in home base or in base camp. "Verily, verily, I say unto you, He that believeth on me, the works that I do shall he do also; and greater works than these shall he do; because I go unto my Father" (John 14:12). It is true that we see healings, deliverances, and other miracles, and we are so very grateful for these. But deep in your heart, you still know there is more God has for us, and you long for it.

I asked a friend once why she thought more people did not pursue the higher realms of God. Her simple answer was, "They are not interested." Upon reflection, I realized that she was correct. Life has a way of growing weeds in your garden. You get so busy doing other things that God's desires get pushed aside. What a pity!

What was it in the life of Jesus that caused the Father to "heal them all" through Him? What caused Him to walk on the water and operate in all the gifts of the Spirit, etc.? A careful look at Luke 4 gives us insight into the answer.

"And Jesus being <u>full of the Holy Ghost</u> returned from Jordan, and was <u>led by the Spirit</u> into the wilderness" (Luke 4:1).

"And Jesus returned <u>in the power of the Spirit</u> into Galilee…" (Luke 4:14).

"<u>The Spirit of the Lord is upon me</u>…" (Luke 4:18).

Here, we see clearly that Jesus was full of the Holy Ghost, led by the Spirit, and was operating in the power of the Spirit. Therefore, our first steps towards doing the works that He did must also be to be 1) full of the Spirit, 2) led by the Spirit, and 3) operating in the power of the Spirit.

A glass can't be full of water if it is already half full of dirt. For any vessel to be <u>full</u> of something, it first has to be emptied of everything else that is in it. For Jesus to be <u>full</u> of the Holy Spirit, he first had to be emptied of self-will. He repeatedly verifies that this has happened in His life.

* "Jesus saith unto them, My meat is to do the <u>will</u> of him that sent me, and to finish his work" (John 4:34).

* "<u>I do not seek or consult My own will</u>—<u>I have no desire to do what is pleasing to Myself</u>,… but only the <u>will</u> and pleasure of the Father Who sent me" (John 5:30b AMP).

* "For I came down from heaven, <u>not to do mine own will</u>, but the <u>will</u> of him that sent me" (John 6:38).

So Jesus was emptied of self-will and had no desire to do anything but the perfect will of the Father at all times. For the life of Christ to be freely flowing through us, we must arrive at that same place—desiring to please the Father above all else. Frank Sinatra sang a song that said, "I did it my way." Our goal is the exact opposite of that—namely, to do it God's way, and have no will of our own in the matter.

There is only one sure way to be emptied of self-will, and that is to be willing to follow Jesus out of base camp and into the unknown climb up "the valley of the shadow of death." Even though most are content to stay where they are, there are a few that will desire to follow Jesus even higher. There must be more than they have experienced in this "base camp," and they will not be satisfied until they have entered into the fullness of what God has for them. So those few souls that will not be deterred will begin yet another adventure with Jesus as they follow Him higher.

When reading the 23rd Psalm, most people assume that "the valley of the shadow of death" means physical death and that we won't be afraid of dying because He is with us. Of course, that is true. But there is another kind of death that we must experience while still alive if we are to arrive at God's high plateau. As we have discovered, that is death to self (self-will). Jesus said "If any man will come after me, let him deny himself, and take up his cross daily, and follow me" (Luke 9:23). And again, Jesus said, "He that taketh not his cross, and followeth after me, is not worthy of me" (Matt. 10:38). So clearly, Jesus is saying that there is a cross, a death to self-will, which is essential if we want to attain to all God has in store for us. Paul expressed it like this: "I am crucified with Christ and it is no longer I that lives, but Christ lives in me, and the life that I now live in the flesh, I live by the faith of the Son of God who loved me and gave Himself for me" (Gal. 2:20).

This really makes a lot of sense if you think about it. God is not willing to pour out His glory into a vessel polluted with mounds of flesh or self-will. We must be willing to say like John the Baptist, "He must increase, but I must decrease" (John 3:30). Every human being starts off full of self-will. Look at any toddler who will jerk a toy away from another child, and say, "Mine!" They want their way, and many will throw tantrums if they don't get it. Some continue to do this even as adults.

Emptying self-will from one's life first requires a desire to do so. It then requires daily awareness of what the Spirit of God is saying and desiring, so you can make continual decisions to do it His way and not your own. I don't want you to think this is complicated, for it is not. It is very simple—simply make your will subservient to His will, every day in every way. Yes, this requires a close relationship with the Holy Spirit. Actually, having this closeness should be a very high priority in our lives because He is the member of the Godhead that is with us at all times, who will never leave us or forsake us, as Jesus promised. He is the One who will lead us into all truth. He is the One who knows the mind of God and can convey it to us. Every feat of power that was done in the life of Jesus was done through the power of the Holy Spirit, and it will be the same with us.

We face an uphill climb as Jesus leads us into this valley of death to self-will. Some would feel that it would be easier to die a physical death than to die to your own will. After all, our entire lives we have been accustomed to attempting to have things done the way we want them. Our goal now becomes to have everything God's way. This is essential if a person wants to be used as an unfettered, unrestricted instrument in the hand of God. God won't continually be wrestling with you over whose will (yours or His) will prevail. He must know that you will always do His will, no matter what your personal feelings are about the situation. You will be tried over and over concerning this until He is assured that you will **always** do what He says.

I heard a story about William Branham that comes to mind in regards to this total abandonment of your own will.

William Branham was on a plane, headed to a speaking engagement, when the weather turned bad, and the plane had to be diverted to another city. They put passengers up in a hotel overnight and told them to be ready at a certain time the next morning to get a ride to the airport to catch a plane to their original destination. Branham got up the next morning and thought he had just enough time to walk to the post office and mail a letter before the transit arrived for the plane. He walked out the hotel door and started walking to his right toward the post office when the Spirit said to him, "Turn around 180 degrees, and walk the opposite direction." In obedience to the Spirit, he did so. He kept walking in that new direction farther and farther away from his ride to the airport. The Spirit told him to continue walking in what seemed to be the wrong direction.

He crossed a railroad track and came to some small houses. A woman was leaning on the front gate of one of these houses and said, "Good morning parson." He replied, "How did you know I was a parson?" She explained that her son lay near death in her house, and she had been praying for him in the middle of the night. The Lord told her that the next morning a parson would come walking by her house wearing a grey suit. She was to ask him in, and he would lay hands on her son, and he would be healed. Branham followed her into the small house and found a young man near death lying on a bed. He prayed the prayer of faith and then left, arriving back at the hotel just in time to catch his ride to the airport.

Branham's behavior impresses me. He could have argued with God, saying that if he walked the opposite direction and kept walking, he would miss his plane and therefore, miss his speaking engagement. That sounds like a logical argument, but God is not interested in us doing what seems right to us. He is interested in obedience to His will, one hundred percent of the time. If He cannot trust us to obey, how can He entrust us with the weightier things of God like signs, wonders, and miracles? If you had a chest full of gold worth one hundred million dollars, would you entrust it into the hands of someone who only obeyed you fifty percent of the time or when it seemed logical to them? Of course not! God is not interested in your IQ. He only cares about your "I will!"

So the purpose of the "valley of the shadow of death" is to help us die to self as Jesus did and as Paul did. Only then can God <u>know</u> that we will do His will, because we have none of our own left. It requires a deep desire on our part to crucify our flesh every time the Spirit calls it to our attention. It also requires us to do whatever the Lord says, whenever He says to do it, with no regard to what people will think or how embarrassing it might be. That pride is a part of our flesh that must be crucified.

Two observations come to mind concerning our climb up the valley.

The first: Every weight must be left behind. The climber on Mt. Everest must leave his wardrobe, his armchair, his TV, etc., because he cannot make even the smallest part of the climb with anything that is not absolutely essential. In like manner, we must leave behind the things of the flesh and the world and have a oneness of purpose—namely, to reach the plateau of God's promises that lies ahead. Nothing should be more important to us in our lives. Obviously, we have to carry on our daily lives with family and work, etc. However in our hearts, we are still seeking God first and foremost. Obeying Him and being pleasing to Him is our fervent desire, and nothing is more important to us than that.

"No man that warreth entangleth himself with the affairs of this life; that he may please him who hath chosen him to be a soldier" (2 Tim. 2:4).

The second: Every moment, we must keep our focus on Jesus. He is the only one who knows the way to the plateau of promise. He is our only source of protection and provision. We must not let Him out of our sight. We know that He never leaves us or forsakes us. We know that His eyes are on us, and His ears open to hear us. His focus is not the issue here. Our focus is the issue. We cannot afford to be distracted and pulled off course by anything.

It reminds me of performing eye surgery, which I have done most of my life. During this intricate surgical procedure, you are viewing the eye through a very high powered magnification (zoom) lens. You cannot lose your focus for one second or the patient's sight may be compromised forever. Focus, focus, focus…it is absolutely critical. Once, I was in the middle of removing a cataract from a patient's eye when the very large, heavy door right behind my head slammed shut with a huge bang. Everyone in the room jumped or jerked at the loud unexpected sound, but I could not afford to lose my focus. I did not move my eyes, my hands or my body. I kept on working as if nothing had happened. More important than focus in eye surgery is focus on Jesus as we walk through every day of our lives.

Plateau of Promise:

As we have said, the main objective as we climb up the mountain through the valley of the shadow of death is to die to our own self-will. As our self-will is crucified, the life of Christ is formed in us more and more by the Holy Spirit. The goal is to reach the place where Jesus walked with no desire to accomplish His own will. That is the way He walked on the plateau of promise, and that is the way we must walk to live there also.

We must be led of the Holy Spirit at all times as Jesus was. And we must be completely obedient to His leading so that He can trust us with His holy anointing. The conflict between our will and God's will must <u>not</u> be present to live on the plateau of promise. The Holy Spirit must have tested and tried us until He knows for sure that we will <u>always</u> do what He says, whether it makes sense to us or not. How much sense does it make to spit in the dirt, and put the mud you made in a blind man's eyes? Yet that is exactly what the Spirit told Jesus to do; so that is exactly what Jesus did—in perfect obedience as always. Jesus was not concerned about what people would think about Him or how crude it must seem to spit in the dirt. All He cared about was pleasing the Father and obeying Him. And of course, that perfect obedience released the power of God to heal the blind eyes.

Here is a very important point to understand: It was the power of the Holy Ghost flowing unhindered through the man Jesus that healed the sick and raised the dead. Jesus, the carpenter from Nazareth, did no miracles for thirty years until the day that he was baptized in the Jordan River by John the Baptist. At that time, the Holy Ghost descended upon Him as a dove, bringing to Him the power of God to do the works that He did. As we have learned from Luke chapter four, it is very clear that it was the Holy Spirit that led Jesus, filled Him, and anointed Him with power. It was the <u>Spirit's power</u>, working through Jesus, not the power of the human man, Jesus of Nazareth.

Until that day at the Jordan River when Jesus was filled with the Holy Spirit, He did no signs, wonders or miracles. The reason it is important for us to understand this is because Jesus said we would do the same works He did. That will be done through us by the same Holy Spirit that did the miracles through Jesus. Jesus was and still is the Son of God, but when He was on the earth, he was operating as a human being, filled with the limitless power of the Holy Spirit. So, as we are emptied of our stinking flesh (self-will), and the Spirit is given the opportunity to fill up that vacated space within us with His presence and power, then the same works the Spirit did through Jesus will be manifested through us. That is our highest goal. That is living on the plateau of promise as Jesus did.

Paul said, "… this one thing I do, forgetting those things which are behind, and reaching forth unto those things which are before, I press toward the mark for the prize of the high calling of God in Christ Jesus" (Phil. 3:14). If one can press on as Paul did, persevere through the arduous task of dying to their own will, and prove to God that they are trustworthy, then the life of Christ can begin to be manifested through them. Part of what Jesus prayed was, "I in them, and thou in me, that they may be made perfect in one; and that the world may know that thou hast sent me…" (John 17:23). Only Jesus can do the works we read about in the gospels. The only hope of glory on this earth will be Christ in you, doing those same works (Col. 1:27). That is the life we can look forward to as we come through the valley of the shadow of death and are lifted by grace onto the **plateau of promise**.

Jesus Needs a Body

The reality that **Jesus needs a body** began dawning in my spirit many years ago when I read about Jesus coming to Kenneth E. Hagin to teach him about the demonic realm. While Jesus was speaking to Hagin, a demon looking like a monkey caused a dark cloud to come between them, so Hagin could no longer see Jesus, but he could hear Him. Next the demon started yelling yakety-yak, yakety-yak in a shrill voice. Now Hagin could no longer see or hear Jesus. He was very disturbed by this because he was missing what Jesus was saying. He kept wondering why Jesus didn't do something about this demon. Finally, Hagin had tolerated it as long as he could, and he commanded the demon to be quiet in Jesus' name. It fell to the floor like a sack of salt and started whining like a whipped pup and shaking all over.

Hagin could now see and hear Jesus again, and he asked Him why He had not gotten rid of the demon. Jesus replied, "<u>If you hadn't done something about that, I couldn't have</u>." That totally demolished Hagin's theology on the subject. He told the Lord he must have heard Him wrong, so Jesus repeated His answer. Hagin couldn't believe the Lord's statement, so he asked Jesus a third time. "You didn't say You couldn't; You said You wouldn't, didn't You?" Jesus replied emphatically, "No, I didn't say I wouldn't; I said, <u>I couldn't</u>." Hagin told the Lord he would not believe that unless He could prove it to him from the Bible. Jesus was happy to comply with that request and pointed out several scriptures.

*One was Matthew 28:18 where Jesus in His resurrected form had said, "All power is given unto Me in heaven and in earth." He told Hagin that power meant <u>authority</u>. He told him not to stop reading there, for the next verse says, "Go ye therefore, and teach all nations...." Jesus explained that by that statement, He had <u>delegated His authority on the earth</u> to the church. (This makes sense because He had already told us in Luke 10:19 that we have power over all the power of the enemy, and nothing shall by any means hurt us.)

*Jesus also quoted James 4:7, "Resist the devil and he will flee from you." Flee means to run away from a situation as in terror, which shows that you have <u>dominion</u> over the devil.

*"Neither give place to the devil" (Eph. 4:27). This means don't let the devil have any place in you; don't let him have an opportunity or a foothold, which means you have <u>authority</u> over him.

*Another scripture Jesus quoted was Mark 16:17. "And these signs shall follow them that believe; In My name shall they cast out devils...." Jesus explained, "That means that in My name they will exercise <u>authority</u> over the devil. I delegated My authority over the devil to the church, and **I can work only through the church**, for I am the Head of the church." Note that we are the ones speaking to the devil in the name of Jesus, but the power to enforce our words comes from Jesus within us. **Jesus needs a body.**

In fact, Jesus pointed out that nowhere in the New Testament were we told to pray to God to do anything about the devil. "To pray against the devil is a waste of time. I've done all I'm ever going to do about the devil," Jesus said. This shocked Hagin, who thought about all the time he had wasted in prayer about the devil. We are the ones to whom Jesus has given authority. We are the ones that are designated to rule. In Matthew 10:1 and 10:8, Jesus specifically tells **us** to "cast out devils."

The point we need to see from this is that Jesus specifically said, "If you hadn't done something about that, I couldn't have." Jesus is saying He had no ability to act until Hagin spoke to the demon in His name. The unspoken corollary to that is, "Since **you did** do something about that, therefore, **I could** do something about it."

Jesus had already told us in Matthew 16:19, "And I will give unto thee the keys of the kingdom of heaven: and whatsoever thou shalt bind (lock, forbid) on earth shall be bound in heaven: and whatsoever thou shalt loose (unlock, permit) on earth shall be loosed in heaven." As soon as we act on His word, then He moves with His power, accomplishing what we have believed and spoken.

That leaves no room for doubt that the responsibility for dealing with the demonic on this earth is squarely ours. If we do not dominate the devil in the name of Jesus, he will not be dominated. That is why he has free reign in the lives of so many people, including Christians, because they do nothing to stop him. "Be sober, be vigilant; because your adversary the devil, as a roaring lion, walketh about, seeking whom he may devour" (1 Peter 5:8). If people are ignorant about the devil, they are easy prey for him. But the next verse says, "Whom resist steadfast in the faith...." You couldn't resist the devil if you didn't have authority over him. However, you do have authority over him, so you can and must resist him. "My people are destroyed for lack of knowledge" (Hos.4:6).

So you see, **Jesus needs a body** that He can work through, a body that is knowledgeable concerning the demonic. You have to know His word, believe His word, and act on it in order to be victorious over the devil.

I want to go back to a statement the Lord made to Hagin, "I've done all I'm ever going to do about the devil." Let's take a walk through the Bible to see the basis for that statement.

*1 John 3:8 states, "For this purpose the Son of God was manifested, that he might destroy the works of the devil." In this verse, God tells us why He sent Jesus to the earth.

*In Hebrews 2:14, God says, "Forasmuch then as the children are partakers of flesh and blood, He also himself likewise took part of the same; that through death he might destroy him that had the power of death, that is, the devil." Here, He tells us that Jesus had to take on flesh like ours so that, through His death, He could defeat the devil who had the power of death.

*Ephesians 4:9-10 tell us that after His crucifixion, Jesus first descended into the lower parts of the earth (hell) before ascending far above all heavens.

*Colossians 2:15 tells us what Jesus did while in hell. "And having spoiled principalities and powers, he made a show of them openly, triumphing over them in it (the cross)." Making a show of them openly is like a conqueror that strips the defeated enemies to the waist, chains them all together in a long line, and then parades them through town, humiliating them in view of everyone.

*In Revelation 1:18, Jesus states that He has the keys of hell and the grave. I can just see Him leading the parade of Satan and his defeated devils, holding the keys of hell and death above His head and shaking them with a big smile saying, "Look what I have." All of our enemies are defeated through Christ Jesus and His shed blood. We no longer have to fear death or any attack of the enemy in life because we have been given complete dominance over Satan and his imps from hell, in Jesus' name. Hallelujah!

*After totally defeating Satan, He ascended into heaven. "<u>Far above all principality, and power, and might, and dominion</u>, and every name that is named, not only in this world, but also in that which is to come: And hath put all things under his feet…" (Eph. 1:21-22).

*The good news for us is that God has given us joint seating with Christ (Eph. 2:6), which also puts us far above all principalities, power, might, dominion, and every name that is named. If we are assured of that position in our hearts and function from that stance, the devils tremble when we come on the scene in the name of Jesus. They know that <u>we know who we are in Him</u>.

So you see, Jesus has done everything He is ever going to do about the devil, just like He told Hagin. Jesus has totally defeated Satan and has passed that dominion on to us. It is now up to us to exercise that dominion that we possess. As we bind the enemy with our words, then the gate is open for the Holy Spirit to flow forth with all the power in the universe and accomplish what we have spoken. **Jesus needs a body** to speak through. He will do the rest!

A beautiful example of our dominance over Satan comes from the life of Smith Wigglesworth. A family living 200 miles away from him sent an urgent request for help. Their daughter was possessed by demons, and they were desperate. Wigglesworth came as they requested. He was led down a hallway and up two flights of stairs, arriving at a closed door. The father opened the door and shoved Wigglesworth in, quickly closing the door behind him.

In the room was a young, frail girl held down by five men. When she saw Wigglesworth, the power of the demonic forces inside of her enabled her to tear loose from the five men. She lunged forward, glaring at Wigglesworth and saying, "You can't cast me out." He answered, "<u>Jesus can, and He is in me</u>." He remembered 1 John 4:4, which says, "Greater is He that is in you, than he that is in the world." Wigglesworth knew that Christ was in him, so he commanded the demons, saying, "Come out in the name of Jesus." Immediately thirty-four demons came out, giving their names as they fled away. The girl was instantly in her right mind. She went down the stairs and had dinner with her family.

The point I want you to see is that Jesus needed the man, Wigglesworth, to speak the command to the demons in His name. But it was entirely the <u>power</u> of Jesus that made them flee. Jesus is always the One with the power, but He needs a person to speak the commanding words. **Jesus needs a body**.

That is the way we should all respond when faced with demons—filled with complete assurance that we have dominion over them in Jesus' name. Acts 10:38 comes to my mind. "How God anointed Jesus of Nazareth with the Holy Spirit and with power: who went about doing good, and healing all that were <u>oppressed of the devil</u>; for God was with him." "As He is, so are we in this world" (1 John 4:17). The same Holy Ghost is in us that was in Jesus, and He wants to do the same things through us that He did through Jesus. All He needs is a yielded body, hopefully like yours.

Christ in Us:

The second thing that influenced my thinking along these lines was an experience a man named James had. James was carried away by the Spirit to a foreign country. He was placed on a dusty terrain with Jesus by his side. There were people with all kinds of sicknesses and deformities all around them. As they walked along, a crippled, emaciated man with no sign of recognition in his eyes was lying at the feet of Jesus. Suddenly, it was as if James was looking through the eyes of Jesus, and the man was lying at his feet. It was as if Jesus had stepped into James or vice versa. Jesus was choosing to work through James' body, but all the power was definitely from the Lord. As James reached out his hand to the crippled man, he noticed it was also the hand of Jesus, like the Lord's hand was in his hand. Within ten seconds, the man was standing before James/Jesus, whole in body and mind and praising God.

Each time James reached out to someone in need, it would be Jesus' hand. Phenomenal miracles were taking place. One person had no arms or legs, he only had a torso. As he reached out his/Jesus' hand, all of the man's limbs grew out within a few seconds, and he was filled with joy. Another spectacular miracle was when Jesus/James reached out his hand, and conjoined twins were instantly separated and ran about with glee. Blind eyes were opened, deaf ears could hear, tumors disappeared, impaired bodies were made whole; any ailment you could think of was cured within fifteen seconds.

Jesus was then outside James' body again and standing by his side. He said, "**Am I not God? Am I not Creator? Is anything too difficult for Me?**" James then found himself back at home with his wife, dusty and exhausted.

About two years after first reading this, the Spirit pointed out to me that as all the healing miracles were taking place, Jesus was doing them <u>through James' body</u>. The two had become one flesh (Eph. 5:31), but it was James' flesh and Jesus' power. Before the healing miracles started, and after they stopped, Jesus was <u>outside</u> James' body, but while they were happening, Jesus was <u>inside</u> James' body. In other words, **Jesus needed a body** to work through. I also realized that Jesus did no healings while in His resurrected body as He had done when He had a physical body before His crucifixion. Apparently, He needed a physical body (whether His own or someone else's) through which to do healing miracles.

Raised from the Dead:

An experience by a woman named Clarice added even more clarity to what I was being shown. She was ministering in a church when the pastor fell dead on the podium. The paramedics came and tried to resuscitate him to no avail. The Lord spoke to Clarice, telling her to raise him from the dead. Her response was, "You go raise him from the dead." The Lord's next comment is the thing that solidified my thinking about Jesus needing a body. He said to her, "**I can't go over there. Nothing manifests in this dimension without a body. <u>You</u> take me over there.** <u>You</u> just put your hand on him and <u>say</u>, 'I bind the spirit of death, and I release resurrection life.'" There it was—Jesus Himself saying what I had already come to understand. **Jesus needs a body**. Thank you Jesus for such a strong confirmation!

Jesus needed <u>her legs</u> to walk over to the body. He needed <u>her hand</u> to touch the body; He needed <u>her mouth</u> to take authority over death and release life. Jesus could not have done any of those things because He no longer had a physical body. But when He found a human being that would obey His instructions, then His power could accomplish the resurrection. This is extremely clear to me, as I pray it is to you, because He wants to use our bodies to live His life through.

Clarice went to the dead body, laid her hand on it, and began to pray in tongues. Jesus interrupted her and said, "What are you doing?" She told Him she was praying. He said, "I didn't tell you to do that." He said that she was being like a car with the gear in park and the motor being revved—she was going nowhere. He reiterated His instruction to her. She then obeyed, went to the body, laid her hand on it, and said, "I bind the spirit of death, and I release resurrection life." At those words from Clarice's mouth, the power of God was released, and Jesus raised the pastor from the dead. All He needed was a body willing to obey Him.

Another important point to see through this example is how specific the command of Jesus was, and any deviation from that command was not only unacceptable, it had no effectiveness. We must listen to His words carefully, and try our best to do exactly what He tells us to do. **He needs a body** that carries out His word with precision.

The Lord pointed out to me that He used a person in every miracle of healing that I cited in Chapter 4. Let's look back at them.

- God used a <u>woman evangelist</u> to pray for Ronald Cohen's eye, and consequently, God enabled him to see through an empty socket.

- God used Evangelist <u>A.A. Allen</u> to pray for Gene Mullinax who had a missing lung and several ribs that had been surgically resected. Instantly, God replaced the lung and ribs at the prayer of the evangelist.

- God used <u>me</u> to speak the resurrection power of Jesus into a severely crippled woman who arose and was able to run around the church like a gazelle.

- God sent <u>Beatrice</u> from Maryland to Las Vegas to pray for a woman that He would show her. When she found Gertrude Ticer near death in the hospital, she prayed and fasted for three days, and spoke anointed words to her about receiving her healing, which opened the door for Jesus to raise Gertrude up.

Each one of us can be used of God to facilitate His miracle-working power. **All Jesus needs is YOUR yielded body.**

Immersed in Jesus

Ezekiel 47 describes a river that flows out from beneath the throne of God. This river brings life to everything that it touches. We commonly think of this river as the river of the Holy Ghost because Jesus said, "Out of his belly shall flow rivers of living water. This He spake of the Holy Ghost..." (John 7:38-39). An angel takes Ezekiel to the bank of the river and proceeds to measure 1000 cubits to a place where the river is ankle deep. He then measures another 1000 cubits to an area that is knee deep. He measures still another 1000 cubits, and the river is waist deep. The next 1000 cubits brought him to water too deep to cross on foot. One must swim beyond that point.

Wading:

There will always be people that stand on the bank and never get one toe wet. However, the thought came to me that the first three measurements bring a person to places where his feet are still on the ground since the water is only ankle deep, knee deep, and waist deep. That means that anyone in these three locations is still in control of their lives. They can choose to turn around and get out of the water, walk to more shallow water or go wherever they want. The river has no control over them. If the river is the Holy Ghost, then He has no control over them. It is good for them to be in the water, for being in the river, even a little bit, is better than not being in the river at all.

But our goal as Christians is to be led of the Holy Ghost at all times. He is the one who should be in complete control of us. Some people are afraid to give up their autonomy, their control. They still want to do things their way. They will follow the Spirit's leading to some degree, unless He wants to do something contrary to their own self-will. Then they will balk like a donkey and say in their hearts, "This is far enough. I want to do it my own way." They think and act this way despite the fact that it limits being used of the Lord. God tells us how the flesh battles the Spirit, and the Spirit battles the flesh. Those two are at odds with one another (Gal. 5:17). You get to decide which one will win out in your life.

Swimming:

Then I thought about the swimmer. He was brave enough to get his feet off of the ground. However, since he can swim, he is still in total control. This might be a category of people who understand the power in the name of Jesus and use that authority, yet they still want to be in control of their own lives, and "do their own thing." Jesus told us about people like that in Matthew 7:21-23 (NIV). "Not everyone who says to me, 'Lord, Lord,' will enter the kingdom of heaven, but only he who <u>does</u> the will of my Father who is in heaven. Many will say to me on that day, 'Lord, Lord, did we not prophesy in your name, and in your name drive out demons and perform many miracles?' Then I will tell them plainly, 'I never knew you. Away from me, you evildoers!'"

Of course there are many fine people swimming in the waters of the Spirit that are obeying God and being fruitful in the kingdom of God. The Spirit will use these consecrated people to whatever extent they will yield to Him. Yet there are other places in this river that could make them even more useful to God.

Floating:

One day many years ago, the Lord showed me that He would like me to be more like a piece of wood thrown into this river. The wood would float with no will of its own, no agenda. It would go wherever the river took it. It could be taken into an area of still water to rest or be taken over the rapids and be banged into rocks (like knocking some flesh out of a person). The piece of wood would have no control over its destiny. That would be controlled by the river, which is the Holy Spirit. The piece of wood would simply <u>float</u>.

I can think of many other examples where Jesus would be in complete control. For instance, if you had a boat, and you gave it to Jesus, then it would become His boat. You would be invited to sit in the back of the boat, prop your feet up, and enjoy the scenery. Jesus would be at the helm deciding where to go and how fast to travel. He would be responsible for putting gasoline in it, buying insurance for it, and providing all the necessary upkeep on the boat. In other words, nothing about that boat would be your concern because it is not your boat. You would not be in control any more than that piece of wood would be in control floating down the river. (Think of that boat as <u>your life</u> given to Jesus.)

At one time, I was looking to buy property in Colorado. I had in my mind what I thought would be ideal. On several occasions, I traveled to Colorado looking at various properties. I prayed a prayer I often pray when

I am not sure of God's perfect will in a matter. I asked Him to open the door and make it easy if I found a property that was His choice for me. On the other hand, I asked Him to shut the door so tightly that no man could open it, if a property was not His will. I really trusted Him to do this for me.

So I kept looking and actually was prepared to make an offer on three occasions. Each time the door would close at the last minute. Finally, He made it very clear that I was not to buy property in Colorado, at least not at that time.

I want you to see how that is like floating in the river because I was not in control of where or when to buy. I had specifically asked Him to be in control of that, and He was. I am very grateful to God for guiding and directing me and keeping me out of trouble in all of life's decisions. He will do that for anyone who will allow Him to make the decisions and then obey Him, even if it is against your personal desires. He certainly knows what is best for us. Often what we think is best turns into a mess if we force our own will. So the point is to float and let the river (God) be in control of your every move.

Immersed in Jesus:

One day, Jesus said to me, "I am the river." That came as a surprise to me, even though it shouldn't have. We think of the river as the Holy Spirit, which we already mentioned. We also know from Psalms 46:5 that God is in the midst of the river. However, I had never thought of Jesus <u>being</u> the river. This one statement from the Lord changed everything in my thinking.

He showed me a vision of a person (let's name him Joe) being immersed in the river, which is the same thing as being immersed in Jesus. This vision was a graphic illustration of what I had been desiring all my life. It was a picture of what it would be like on the plateau of promise. It demonstrated what Paul talked about in Galatians 2:20 where he says, "I no longer live, but <u>Christ lives in me</u>." And at the same time it was a picture of Acts 17:28, which says, "<u>In Him we live</u> and move and have our being."

In the vision He gave me, Joe was in Him, since Jesus is the river. And at the same time the river (Jesus) was flowing into and out of Joe. In other words, <u>He was IN Joe</u>, and <u>Joe was IN Him</u> simultaneously. Wow, at last I could see this clearly. The water of the river was coming down from the throne of God. It was coming into Joe's back, filling every fiber of his being, and freely flowing out of Joe to the world, which is desperate for the life of God that the river provides.

I also want to point out that the life-giving river will also have an effect on Joe himself—on his health, his thinking, his spiritual life, on every part of his being. He will live in more continuous glory than most people have ever dreamed of. Everyone that loves God would love to be where Joe is and feel what he feels. Actually, that "secret place" (Ps. 91:1) is available to anyone that is willing to pay the price and be crucified of their own self-will.

There is another facet of this river that will be of tremendous benefit to Joe. It is found in Psalm 46. The first set of terrible circumstances is found in verses 2 and 3, "Therefore will not we fear, though the earth be removed, and though the mountains be carried into the midst of the sea; ...."

The second set of bad circumstances is found in verse 6. "The heathen raged, the kingdoms were moved: he uttered his voice, the earth melted." Sandwiched in between these two sets of catastrophic circumstances, we find the benefits of being immersed in the river in verses 4 and 5. "There is a river, the streams whereof shall make <u>glad</u> ... God is in the midst of her; <u>she shall not be moved</u>...."

This passage tells us that the water of this river will make us glad, even in the midst of turmoil. It also tells us that our God is in the midst of the river, so if we are in the river with Him, we will not be moved—no matter what circumstances are taking place in the world around us. Immersed in this river is definitely the place we need to be—full of gladness, with God, immovable.

Let me refer again to the letter Kathryn Kuhlman once wrote me. "There is really no limit to what God can do with a person, providing that one will not touch the glory. God is still waiting for one who will be more fully devoted to Him than anyone who has ever lived; who will be <u>willing to be nothing</u> that Christ may be all; who will grasp God's own purposes and taking His humility and His faith, His love and His power—**without hindering,** <u>let</u> God do great things."

In the vision Jesus showed me, there were **no hindrances** to His flowing through Joe. It was as easy for Him to go through Joe in the river as it was for Him to go through a wall with His resurrected body.

This was the clearest picture of ministry I had ever envisioned because it was no longer Joe (or you) that had anything to do with ministering. You were simply the body that the Holy Ghost would take to a place for Jesus to flow through. It was all Jesus! You were just the body He happened to be using at that moment, through which He would heal, deliver, preach, teach, prophesy, hug or anything else He wanted to do.

Do you see it? This concept is totally liberating from a ministry standpoint. If we can all become immersed in the river of Jesus, and let Him flow freely through us without hindrance, the entire world will change.

Let's go back to the river with Ezekiel for a moment. We have seen five categories of people in relationship to the river.

1) Those standing on the bank with not a drop of water on them. Since the Holy Spirit gives us the power to be a witness (Acts 1:8), these people have little usefulness in God's kingdom.

2) People wading ankle deep, knee deep, and waist deep into the Holy Spirit.

3) People swimming in the river.

4) People floating in the river like pieces of wood.

5) People immersed in Jesus.

The categories of wading, swimming, and floating all have something in common: They are all partially in the water and partially out of the water. We know that the water represents God the Father, God the Son, and God the Holy Spirit. Being out of the water represents the world and the flesh. So people who are partially out of the water still have cords of attachment to the world that are holding them up. As long as they have these cords to the world, they can never be totally immersed in Jesus.

This is what God has to say about our cords to the world and the flesh: "For those who walk according to the flesh set their minds on the things of the flesh, but those who walk according to the Spirit, the things of the Spirit. For the mind set on the flesh (which is sense and reason without the Holy Spirit) is death, but the mind set on the Spirit is life and peace; because the mind set on the flesh is hostile toward God; for it does not subject itself to the Law of God (the Word of God), for it is not even able to do so; and those who are in the flesh can not please God" (Rom. 8:5-8 NASB).

Sometimes the world has cords on us that we do not even recognize. Not long ago, the Lord showed me one last cord that attached me to the things of the world. This may sound strange to you, but if you are an avid sports fan you will understand. I had always loved to watch the Dallas Cowboys play football. I never wanted to miss one moment of a game. When I was doing surgery, if there was a short lull while they were getting the next patient ready for surgery, I would go to the doctor's break room, find the sports page in the paper, and read all about the players or the projections for the next game. If I had to miss a game, I would record it, and watch it later. If they played well and won the game, I might watch it twice.

The Lord showed me that this sport was a cord that had too much of a pull on me, and it must be cut. When He showed that to me, I cut it off immediately, and never again watched a game or read anything about the team. It was now dead to me.

If we will ask the Holy Spirit to show us any cords to the world that are not pleasing to Him, then He will reveal them to us. Of course, our response should be to quickly cut them. We do not want anything in our lives that is not pleasing to our Father, nothing that is counterproductive to His perfect will for us. Our goal is to be set free from the influences of the world. Like Jesus, we are "in it" but don't want to be "of it" (possessed by it). Obedience is better than sacrifice.

Remember when Jesus said of the devil, "He has nothing in me" (John 14:30). In other words, Jesus had no cords to the world. So the devil could not grab any cords and jerk Jesus around. He had no flesh handles to grab, no flesh floats holding Him up out of the water and into the world. He had been set free from the allure of the world by crucifying His will and yielding totally to the will of God.

"My meat is to <u>do the will</u> of Him that sent me, and to finish His work" (John 4:34).

"The Son is able to do nothing from Himself (of His own accord); but is able to do only what He sees the Father doing..." (John 5:19 AMP).

The Bible says, "As He is, so are we in this world" (1 John 4:17).

"For to me to live IS Christ" (Phil. 1:21).

So if we want our lives to reflect the life of Christ, it is clear that we must cut the cords that still permit the world to influence us or even control us.

It was right after cutting that last cord of football when the Lord showed me about being immersed in Jesus. I would far, far, far rather be <u>in Jesus</u> than engrossed in some football team. The things that we can get attached to can really be so trivial in the whole scheme of things. Can you imagine standing before of the throne of God and Him saying, "How did the Cowboys play yesterday?" Instead I want Him to say, "Well done, My good and faithful servant. You crucified yourself to the world, you brought souls into My kingdom, you spent the time I gave you in the world wisely...enter into the joy of the Lord."

We all need to cut the attachments to the world that hinder us, that hold us out of the river of Jesus. We need to set our goal on being **immersed in**

Him and having Him flow freely though us without hindrance. For only His life is full of power with signs, wonders, and miracles that will draw the lost into the kingdom of God. **Jesus needs a body.** Let it be yours.

Erasing the "I"

One day after teaching me about being immersed in Jesus, the Lord said three words to me, "**Erasing the I.**" He then showed me that inside every human being there is a big letter "I." This of course represents their own will, their own thinking, and their own desires. If a person has reached the point in God where they are immersed in Jesus, it is still possible to have a big "I" inside of them. This is obviously an impediment to the flow of the river through them. Ideally a person would be free of the things of the flesh (the "I"), and therefore, Jesus could flow through them **without hindrance**, as Miss Kuhlman wrote.

The problem is how to erase this big "I" from within us. I have asked the Holy Spirit to do this for me and have seen by vision, the "I" being erased a little at a time. First of all, I believe it has to be a joint venture with the person wanting the "I" erased and, secondly, being willing to do anything and everything as the Holy Spirit leads. We are the blackboard with the "I" written on it. The Holy Spirit is the One with the eraser in His hand. However, He cannot erase anything without our permission and our cooperation. After all, the blackboard is each person's life, and He will not do anything unless we want it done.

Even if a person loves God and wants to be used by Him, his eyes may still be focused on himself by thinking things like: "Am I ready? Am I able? Am I prepared? Am I good enough?" etc. Our focus needs to be on Jesus, not on ourselves, just like Jesus focused on the Father and not on Himself.

Jesus said, "… the Father that dwelleth in me, he doeth the works" (John 14:10). He was focused on the Father, looking only at the Father, depending only on the Father. He was not looking at His own ability, but at the Father's ability. He knew that He was in the Father, and the Father was in

Him. He had that assurance, so there was no need for Jesus to think about the "I." We need the same assurance that we are in Jesus, and Jesus is in us, so we look to His ability, His readiness, and His faith. **Jesus needs a body** that does not have the hindrance that the "I" creates.

Since I have already asked the Holy Spirit to do for me what I am unable to do by myself (erase the "I"), and since I am determined to obey Him in every tiny thing He requires, I now walk by faith that He will do it. Jesus said, "Therefore I say unto you, What things soever ye desire, when ye pray, believe that ye receive them, and ye shall have them" (Matt. 11:24). He also said, "If ye shall ask anything in my name, I will do it" (John 14:14). Jesus is not a liar. So we can be confident that if we do our part, He will certainly do His part in **erasing the "I."**

Chapter 7

Wonders

The Aptitude Test

When I was a freshman in college, I was a math major because I had always loved math. I began to investigate careers in math, and none of them appealed to me. So I decided to take an aptitude test to hopefully get some guidance in a different career direction. If you have never taken an aptitude test, it gives you choices like this, "Would you prefer to 1) read a book, 2) work in the garden, or 3) type a letter?" After making many choices on a variety of subjects, the results are tabulated to help lead you in career decisions. They told me that the results would be reported in three categories. 1) You should seriously consider these careers. 2) You could possibly have aptitude in these careers. 3) You have no aptitude in these careers.

When the results came back, the counselor at the testing and counseling center of the college called me in for a meeting. He started off by being apologetic about the results and said he had never, ever seen a result like this in all of his years of being a counselor. There were **no** results in the middle category. There was **one** result in the top category, namely **MEDICINE**. All the other results were in the last category—not to be considered. His only suggestion was to investigate a career in medicine. This field had never entered my mind. My paternal grandfather was a medical doctor, so I guess I had this aptitude in my genes, but I had never considered it.

I spent the following summer doing an externship at a local hospital. One night, they allowed me to come to surgery and observe my first surgical case. This was very exciting to me, so I rushed to the hospital, not wanting to miss one second of the surgery. It was an emergency surgery on a man who had his finger cut off in a lawn mower accident. They put a cap, gown, mask, and gloves on me (this was exciting too) and then ushered me into the surgical suite. I took one look at the macerated stub of this man's finger sticking up through the drape and almost fainted. I quickly sat down before I fell down. That was the only time in my life that I shied away from surgery. Actually, as it turned out, I loved being a surgeon, but that is getting ahead of my story.

I switched to pre-med as a sophomore, taking a heavy load of science classes—biochemistry, anatomy, physiology, physics, etc. I liked them all, so I continued as a pre-med student. As a junior, I applied to two medical schools. They reviewed my entrance exam scores, my college grades, my recommendations, and then invited me for personal interviews. Afterwards, I was very nervous while I waited for a response from the schools. My entire future hung in the balance of their decisions.

Finally, I got a letter from one of the medical schools. I remember carrying that letter and walking down the sidewalk headed to another class. I was afraid to open it, but too anxious to put it off. So I finally mustered the courage to open that life-changing letter. They had accepted me! I was so thrilled and relieved. I knew I could now be a doctor. I really preferred the other school I had applied to, however, the pressure to get into medical school was now off. Not long after this, I received a letter from my preferred medical school, and they too had accepted me. Wow, my dream had come true!

When I was a teenager, my godly grandfather, who was a Methodist minister, prophesied that I would become a medical missionary. I was a pre-med student at that time and respectfully received his word, but in my heart, I could not imagine that. In retrospect, my grandfather was exactly right. God used that M.D. degree and surgical profession to open doors into countries that were closed to the gospel of Jesus Christ. The Lord even made a way for us to build an eye surgery center in Beijing, China, where we did much free surgery on poor people.

After practicing medicine for forty years and loving it, it is obvious to me that it was the hand of God leading me in the direction He had for my life through that strange, miraculous aptitude test result. What a mighty God we serve!

The Wonder of Doreen

In April of 1994, on one of our trips to China, we visited Xian, an ancient, walled city in western China made famous by the amazing Terracotta Army. This army of approximately eight thousand men was buried with Emperor Qin Shi Huang around 210 B.C., presumably to guard him in his afterlife.

On the wall of Xian, I met a young woman selling items to tourists. One of the ladies with me had told her that I was a doctor. This peaked her interest since her father and brother were also doctors, so she came over to me and started a conversation. Someone took our picture, and I told her I would send her a copy of it. She later told me that other tourists said they would send her a picture, but no one ever did. So she was surprised when I actually sent her a picture as I told her I would. At the time, I never would have guessed that this was a meeting ordained by God to facilitate His purposes for His kingdom and our lives.

As I got to know her better, I found out some interesting things about her life. When she was a small child, the country had gone through some very difficult times—food was scarce and many Chinese were starving to death. Although she was only six years old, she had to go before sunup each morning and stand in a long line for hours to get food for her elderly grandparents to keep them alive. When Doreen was in the fifth grade, schools were closed because of the Cultural Revolution. The government separated her from her family and sent her to the countryside with other children to do farm work with the peasants. There, she slept on a bed of hardened mud and did strenuous manual labor. At fourteen years of age, she joined the army, where she was trained as a nurse. This also had not been an easy life.

As a young adult, Doreen had a strong desire to learn English. Despite the curtailment of her formal education, she was determined to continue learning. She watched as many television programs as she could where English was spoken, so she could hear the language. She got books and studied long hours on her own. She did not know why she had such a desire to learn English. Beyond speaking the language, she had no further goals in mind. It was a driving force within her, but where it would lead, she had no idea. This desire to learn English was so strong that she left her nursing job in her father's clinic and began to sell things to tourists on the wall at Xian. She thought that she could improve her English by speaking to tourists. She had made this job move just two months before the fateful day we met her on the wall.

On our next trip to China, we met with Doreen again. She had been studying ophthalmology on her own for no apparent reason except that it was interesting to her. Her English was amazingly improved in such a short time. I had never met anyone so diligent in studying. Can you imagine yourself learning Chinese from a book with no tutor and at the same time, learning the complicated terminology of a surgical subspecialty in Chinese? That is essentially what Doreen did—**amazing!** Needless to say she is very bright in addition to being extremely diligent.

When I came home to Dallas and had time to reflect on the events of the trip, I realized that it would be very useful to have a bilingual nurse. She could help me during surgery in China and teach ophthalmic duties to other Chinese nurses as we built the surgery center we wanted to create in Beijing. I would first have to bring her to America to train her in my office. I spoke with her on the phone and asked her if she would be interested in doing this. She was elated. In fact, her family told her that she must have misunderstood me when I invited her to come to America. This opportunity was too good to be true!

Little did I know that it was nearly impossible for her to get a visa to come to America. She made several trips from Xian to the American Embassy in Beijing (about a thirty-six hour train trip one way, usually standing up to save money) trying to get a visa, and always being turned down. I told Doreen to meet us in Beijing on our next trip to China. We would go to the Embassy with her, and she would get a visa. I was very emphatic about this because I believed God would make a way where there seemed to be no way. At that point, Doreen didn't really know God and couldn't imagine how we could possibly get her visa. Her previous denials had made this goal seem unreachable.

When we met her in Beijing, we took her to the American Embassy, where we met with a high-ranking official. I explained to him that I needed to train Doreen in America so that she could help us with the work at Glory Eye Center in Beijing, where we would be doing free eye surgery on poor people. God moved with His favor on this official, and he gave her a visa. We had a celebration by buying a fresh pineapple. Doreen cut it, and we ate it with great joy over God's provision. It was a celebration like none other I can remember.

Doreen did come to America, and with that same diligent nature, she learned how to be an ophthalmic technician and a scrub nurse for my eye surgery cases. And I might add, she was excellent at these tasks—much better than many others I have worked with who were born in America.

So over the years, she became part of our team, traveling back and forth between America and China, making blind people see in both countries for the glory of God.

Doreen is now an American citizen, which is a good thing for America and for Doreen. She married a wonderful American man who loves God. She was also able to bring her son, Hu Hu, to America when he was a teenager. It was extremely difficult for him to step into high school classes knowing very little English. However, with his mother's same diligent nature and her continual help, he made top grades. Hu Hu went on to get a master's degree in chemistry and is now working for Exxon Mobile. He married a beautiful Chinese woman, and they have a young son. He is also a deacon in his local church.

In retrospect, Doreen realizes that it was God who gave her the desire to learn English so that He could use her life for His purposes. She and her son are both consecrated Christians and serve God diligently today. It is amazing how God brought them out of a life of darkness, never knowing Jesus, into the light of His kingdom.

Today she is one of my best friends and has been over the decades. We look forward to the day when God sends us back to China to bring the gospel of Jesus Christ to hungry hearts. In fact, God gave Doreen a dream of us entering a "mud hut" like the one she lived in as a child with the peasants. In the hut was a helpless elderly blind woman, lying on a mud bed. We laid hands on her in the name of Jesus. His resurrection power flowed through the woman, and she was able to see again. By the grace of God, we expect to see this dream become a reality in His timing. With God, wonders never cease!

Du Yi Ping (Doreen)

The Watch Miracle

(Written by Geri Morgan)

I want to share this story because I think it is phenomenal. A friend, in Dallas, and her husband were married many years before his death. They never had children, so the two of them shared an unusually close bond. Sadly, he passed away, and one of the things she treasured most was an engraved watch he had given to her. She especially treasured the watch because it was a tangible keepsake that she had left of her memories of him.

After a shopping trip to Dallas one afternoon, she returned home to discover her watch was gone. She had lost it somewhere downtown. Of course, she went back and tried to find it—but to no avail. She even advertised in the Dallas paper but got no response. She was just devastated.

A couple of years went by, and she was reading a heart-touching story in the newspaper about a widow with several children. It was Christmas time, and the children were going to have a very bleak holiday. My friend said God had spoken to her heart to share a small amount of money with this lady. She got the address out of the newspaper, put the money in an envelope, and sent it off to the lady. She never heard anything from the newspaper and didn't really expect to hear anything from the woman.

A year later at Christmas, she received a call from a lady who identified herself as the woman in Midland, Texas, who had received the money. She was calling to thank my friend for what she had done. The money had helped give her children a good Christmas. The lady said she was going to be in Dallas, and although she still didn't have much money, she wanted to take my friend out for lunch in appreciation for what she had done for her children.

They met for lunch and enjoyed a pleasant conversation. The lady began to share a story about being in Dallas several years before that. She said, "You know, I was in downtown Dallas, and I found a watch. You were so very kind to us, and I want to thank you by giving this watch to you." My friend said she knew it was going to be her watch, the one she had lost. Sure enough, it was the watch from her endearing husband with the engraving still on it. An amazing story!

What a miracle God did for my sweet friend. She was faithful to follow the Holy Spirit in her giving. Some might call it a coincidence. I call it an outstanding miracle from the Lover of her soul, Jesus.

One Dieth in His Full Strength

One of my best friends in the world was Ruth Ward Heflin, a powerful woman of God. Geri, Ruth, and I had celebrated the twentieth anniversary of our friendship in Switzerland and France in November of 1999. Ruth was holding meetings in various towns in that area, and we were by her side.

One meeting stands out in my mind in Macon, France. Ruth was not well, but being the Spirit-led world traveler that she was, she was pushing

herself to minister with all the strength she had. She was seated in a chair on the platform behind a microphone, and she began to sing a "new song"...
"It is given unto you to know the mysteries of the kingdom; it is given unto you to know the mysteries of our God."

She sang these words over and over and over until they sank down into the spirits of everyone there. People started standing up and singing it with her, and then they began marching around the large room while singing it. This went on for about an hour without stopping.

Jesus said, "But the hour cometh, and now is, when the true worshippers shall worship the Father in spirit and in truth: for the Father seeketh such to worship him. God is a Spirit: and they that worship him must worship him in spirit and in truth" (John 4:23-24). The Holy Spirit was speaking to the body of Christ through that song. And at the same time, His church was worshipping the Father in Spirit and in truth. What a glorious night! Those words are still ringing inside my spirit as I'm sure they are in the hearts and minds of hundreds of others that were there that night.

When we boarded the plane to fly back to America, Ruth was so weak that she could not walk up the stairs to the plane. They had to lift her onto the plane with one of their machines. She was seated in the aisle seat across from my aisle seat. She was in much pain and asked me to rub her arm. She had been in an auto accident not long before this, and I attributed her weak, painful state to the aftermath of that accident. But as a doctor, many of the things I saw did not add up to that scenario. I had no idea that she was actually dying.

Her parents had founded a Pentecostal camp in Virginia, and that is where she was living at that time. Her father had died, her brother had died, and her mother was in a semi-comatose state. Ruth still tried to run the camp meetings despite her failing condition. She would be taken in a wheelchair to the outdoor "tabernacle" for meetings in the summer. It is said that quitters never win, and winners never quit. Ruth was a winner through and through and by the grace of God, would <u>never</u> quit.

The last time I saw Ruth was in August of the year 2000. She could not stand and could barely move. She stayed in a recliner with several women from the ministry caring for her. Her vision had failed to the point that she could not read her Bible, which grieved her. Being an eye surgeon, I had equipment that I thought might help her see, so I flew to Virginia to do whatever I could. I had a glasses frame that would hold various loose lenses. I tried several strong lenses to see if any of them would allow her to read. Finally, I handed her a Bible with her wearing the strongest lenses I had brought. The Bible fell open spontaneously, and she began to read, **"One dieth in his full strength, being wholly at ease and quiet."** She closed the Bible and put it down. The verse she had read was Job 21:23. No one but God could have had the Bible fall open to that very page, had her eyes fall on that one verse, and given her the momentary ability to read it.

This scripture struck me as being strange at first, since she was not at "full strength" in her body. However, it soon became clear that she was at her "full strength" spiritually, believing God for every moment, as she had done all her life. She was "wholly at ease and quiet" (the NASB says "satisfied") in her spirit. Her life had been overflowing with Jesus since she was a child. She knew her permanent home awaited her. She had been spent for the cause of Christ.

I knew she would soon go to heaven, and she knew that too, although neither of us stated it. I asked her if I could have something of hers to keep. She understood why without saying a word. She gave me some carved elephants that her brother brought back from India. She also gave me three large paintings of Jerusalem. She had hired a local artist to paint them while she was living in Jerusalem. I hung them behind my desk in my medical office and cherished them as something very special from Ruth's heart.

Her parting words to me shortly before she died were, "I love you. I am going to my next assignment. Live in the glory."

I am so grateful that she spoke those words to me. I have tried to live up to her admonition to "live in the glory." To me that means living in the presence of Jesus at all times, for He is the only One who has glory. It involves taking the journey that Paul took and arriving at the destination he described in Galatians 2:20: "I am crucified with Christ: nevertheless I live; yet not I, but <u>Christ liveth in me</u>: and the life which I now live in the flesh I live by the faith of the Son of God, who loved me, and gave himself for me." I am still on the journey toward that full realization.

Ruth died on September 15, 2000. I am certain the Lord greeted her with a smile, saying, "Well done, thou good and faithful servant...enter thou into the joy of thy Lord" (Matt. 25:21).

Ruth Ward Heflin

Chapter 8

Angels

Ski in the Tree

I love to ski, and in my younger years, I did it as often and as fast as possible. One day while skiing down a narrow, winding trail alone, and of course going very fast, I hit a segment of the trail that was solid ice. Before I had a chance to react at all, I found myself in a tree with my face staring at the bottom of my right ski. The hill I was skiing on was very steep, and when I was catapulted from the trail, I was flung in a downhill direction into the top of a tree. I guess you could say into the arms of a tree, as it seemed to have "caught" me! Here I was, "fastened" to this tree limb with no one to help me down. As I pondered the situation, I realized that my leg was bent back on itself sideways like a pretzel, and this was an anatomic position that could only be accomplished if the leg had been broken—but I felt no pain.

109

I calmly unfastened the ski whose bottom was in my face and let the ski drop to the ground. I then reached down and unfastened the other ski from my dangling left leg and let it drop. I then untangled myself from the limb and climbed down from the tree. I retrieved my two skis, put them on, and skied down the rest of the trail. Needless to say, I slowed down lest there be more hiding ice around.

I was truly amazed that I was not hurt in any way—no pain and no broken leg, which certainly should have been the case. I was whole and well to ski another day. I am totally convinced that the angels of God buffered my fall and gave me a gentle landing, not to mention the supernatural fact that my leg was not broken to bits. There is no possible explanation in the natural. As a medical doctor, I knew then as I know now that no one but God can allow a leg to be bent in the direction mine was bent without dire consequences. No one was there to see it but God and me, so no one knows what a miracle this was but the two of us and, of course, the angels He sent to carry out His word over me that day (Hebrews 1:14).

Angel Lifting Power

A longtime friend, Dino Kartsonakis, called me at the end of 2015 and told me of a marble angel that Kathryn Kuhlman had given him. Dino had been the anointed pianist at her crusades. As a gift of appreciation, she had purchased this beautiful, antique marble angel in Beverly Hills, California, and given it to him over forty years before. It was the first gift Miss Kuhlman had ever given him, and he cherished it dearly. The angel was made of solid white marble and stood about five and a half feet tall. It was standing on a pedestal of solid, green marble, which gave it a total height of about nine feet. The angel had its wings spread and was caring for a woman.

Much to my surprise, Dino said the Lord had told him to give that angel to me. This was a huge "seed" he was sowing in obedience to Jesus. Of course, you can never out give God, so Dino is in store for a huge harvest from this "seed."

The statue was so heavy that he had to hire a team of men to wrap it and load it into his vehicle. Dino and his wife, Cheryl, drove from Branson, Missouri, on January 16, 2016, to deliver this angel to us. We had four men waiting to carry the pieces into our house and reassemble them. The green pedestal came in several parts. Each part was very heavy, but manageable. After the pedestal was reassembled, the men lifted the heavy base of the angel onto the pedestal. Now came the hardest part. The entire angel with the woman in his arms was sculpted in one enormous piece of marble. I have no idea what it actually weighs, but I would guess several hundred pounds. The four men tried and tried to lift it the necessary four feet into the air to set it on its base, but failed. Finally, they said to me, "You are going to have to hire movers to lift this. It is too heavy for us to do it."

At this point, I asked them, "Do you believe in prayer?" Their heads nodded, so I prayed and asked the Lord to enable them to lift that angel into place. I then told the angels of God to lift it up for them. You may be wondering about me telling the angels of God to lift the statue. Even though we can't see them, angels are real beings, and they are assigned to us by God to help us with whatever we need.

The Bible tells us, "Are they not all ministering spirits, sent forth to minister <u>for</u> them who shall be heirs of salvation" (Heb. 1:14). Jesus once came to Kenneth E. Hagin and explained that angels are like a waitress in a restaurant. You tell her what you want, and she goes and gets it for you. That simple illustration makes the function of angels very clear. The lifting of the statue would be a demonstration of angels ministering <u>for</u> us, since we are definitely "heirs of salvation" through Jesus Christ.

At the end of the prayer, I told them to now lift it into place. They were willing to try one more time. Much to their surprise, it now seemed much lighter, and they were able to pick it up and set it in place. They were absolutely amazed that the prayer had totally changed their ability to lift the statue.

What a wonderful demonstration to all of us that our God hears and answers prayers. He really does!! This is not some religious theory. Prayer is simply talking to God the way we would talk to another person. We know that He hears us because we come in the name of Jesus. Actually, He wants us to communicate with Him every day in every detail of our lives. After all, He is our Father who loves us beyond our comprehension. He wants us to be healthy, happy, and have all of our needs met—even the need to lift a solid marble statue.

Yesterday, I saw the leader of a construction crew who recently had a party for his workers. He told me that the men involved in lifting the angel were talking about it all during the party. They were in awe over the fact that God made it seem like that marble angel was very much lighter after our prayer. I think that episode made everyone's faith grow and made God more real in everyday life. Thank you, Jesus, for sending angels to lift that marble statue, thereby lifting and strengthening our relationship with You.

Marble Angel

Pear Picking

Once, I bought some land in the countryside that had an old pear tree on it. You could tell that the tree had been there a long time because it was very large. Sadly, no one had cared for it, so it grew very little fruit. The following summer, it did bear a few pears, which were in the very top of the tree. I decided to pick them and take them to my pastor, however, I could not climb high enough to reach them. So I bought a long pole with a basket on the end, which the salesman told me was great for reaching high fruit.

Being young and fearless, I climbed the tree as far as I could and then took out my new "fruit picker." If I stood on a limb on my tip toes and stretched as high as I could reach, I could touch a pear. Wow! As I was straining in this precarious stance, I fell off of the branch, which was about ten feet above the ground and landed flat on my feet with my trusty "fruit picker" still in an upright position in my hand. How in the world did that happen? I understood how I could fall out of the tree; but how could I fall ten feet and land upright on my feet without falling to the ground or even worse breaking my neck? I stood there in shock for a few minutes and then realized that the invisible angels of God were again at work in my behalf, setting me down gently on my feet. They were doing what God had designed them to do.

"For he shall give his angels charge over thee, to keep (guard, defend) thee in all thy ways. They shall bear thee up in their hands, lest thou dash thy foot against a stone" (Psalms 91:11-12).

Thank God for angels! They have saved me from inevitable harm many times.

Angels in Blue Scrub Suits

I have a friend named Alma to whom God gives dreams and visions very frequently. One night, she had a dream of a large RV (motor home) with a man standing by it, wearing a blue scrub suit, which is something that is worn by surgery staff in surgery. She felt like the RV belonged to me, although she did not know that I even had an RV. She also described the way it was painted with designs on the sides and various shades of beige and brown. Her description was exactly the way my RV looked. She did not know for sure what the dream meant, but she felt it indicated I would be taking big trips. Later, I took a picture of my RV and showed it to her. She said that is what the RV looked like in her dream.

About two months later, she had just gone to bed. She was not asleep, but had her eyes closed when the Lord showed her a vision of two huge, muscular men—again in blue scrub suits. They were 9-10 feet tall and had to be angels. As she was looking at them, one of them stepped aside a little bit, showing her that they had me there with them.

I was sharing this vision with a friend, and she said, "They are there to help you with spiritual surgery, just like you had help when you did eye surgery in the natural. That is why they have on blue scrub suits." That was an interesting interpretation of the dream and vision. My friend may be correct. I trust God will show me in due time.

Angel in the Subway

Years ago, Geri and I were in New York City on a Sunday and decided to go to a church that was in a location far north of where we were staying. I had subway maps that had different routes crossing in every direction and looked like spaghetti all tangled up. I had studied them carefully and knew exactly where to get off of one route and transfer to another to reach our destination. The subway routes were well marked at the tracks. I got us to the correct location to catch the northbound train that we needed.

As we were standing by the tracks, I kept watching the time and thinking we were getting later and later for church. I also was rechecking the routes to be sure I had not made any mistakes, when a young man came up to me and asked if I would help him. Despite being pushed for time and wondering why our train had not yet come, I stopped what I was doing and told him I would be glad to help him the best I could. He wanted to go to some far off place. Being from Texas, I knew nothing about where this place was. I studied the maps and finally found how to transfer from one line to another, and to yet another, so he could get to his destination. He thanked me and walked away.

All this time, Geri had been standing there not saying a word, which was very unusual for her. She is very gregarious and will usually strike up a conversation with any stranger and be their friend in ten minutes. When the man walked off, she said, "I am sure glad you helped that man."

"Why?" I asked.

"Because he was an angel, and that was a test for you," she replied.

Geri could sometimes exaggerate about things in the natural, but when it came to spiritual things, she never spoke up unless she was <u>positive</u>. I knew she was serious, and she was right. "Be not forgetful to entertain strangers: for thereby some have entertained angels unawares" (Heb. 13:2). God told us this could happen, and it just did.

I would never have known that he was an angel if Geri had not told me. He looked like a normal human being. God had spoken to Geri in an audible voice years before and told her that she would be "working with the word of knowledge." She could perceive things that no one else could know. I trusted her when she knew something in the Spirit. I was sure glad I had been helpful to that man, despite my own circumstances at the time. Geri said I had passed the test.

By this time, we were really late for church. It wasn't long until a train did come on the tracks, but it was traveling south instead of north. Now I was really confused. A southbound train had just come down a northbound track. I looked at all the signs again. It said <u>for sure</u> that this is the track for the northbound train. We both stood there stunned, wondering what we should do next, when we heard another train coming on the same track. This time it was headed northbound. We got on it, relieved that we were finally headed in the right direction. By the time we got to church, it was half over, but we were just glad to have made it.

What a day it had been. We met an angel, saw a train go the wrong direction on the track, and made it to half of a church service. I wondered what tomorrow would bring. Walking with Jesus is always exciting!

Chapter 9

God's Perfect Timing

The Sale of My Medical Practice

After four years of college, four years of medical school, one year of internship, and three years of residency training in ophthalmology (eye surgery), I was finally prepared to start my own solo practice of medicine in 1970. I absolutely loved my profession. I loved caring for people and helping them with their eye injuries and diseases. Surgery was my favorite part because you could restore sight to a person that was blind or had diminished vision. Patients were ever so grateful, often saying that having the surgery was the best thing that ever happened in their lives.

As the years went by, I still loved taking care of patients; however, the paper work required by the government grew more voluminous, the reimbursement diminished, and the weight of dealing with employees grew heavier. After about thirty-six years, I decided to sell my practice. I contacted a broker, and he sent a number of prospective buyers my way, but no sale was made. Finally, I took my practice off of the market and told the Lord that I would practice medicine as long as He wanted me to, and when it was <u>His perfect timing</u> to sell it, then that would be fine with me. I left the matter entirely in His hands. That release to Him brought great peace to me. I made only one request of Him, and that was to sell it to a consecrated Christian who would maintain it with love and integrity under His guidance.

Shortly after that decision, the building that housed my office for many years was sold. All the doctors leasing space there were told that they had to vacate the building because they planned to build high-rise apartments on that site. Needless to say, this came as an unwanted surprise to me. Now I was forced into finding a new office space and building the interior into the appropriate "eye lanes" and offices that I would need. Specialized movers would have to be hired to move all of my delicate medical equipment, as well as regular movers to move all of my furniture, files, and office equipment. All of this would be at great expense to me at a time when, in my heart, I really wanted to slow down. But I had already put my practice in the hands of the Lord and persisted in leaving it there, trusting Him for all my needs.

About this time, Geri got a word from God that He was going to make my new office a "manger." Like the wise men were led to find Jesus at His birth, God would lead people to my office to find Jesus in this hour. That made me very happy since serving the Lord was the highest goal of my life. I no longer cared about selling the practice. You can read this entire story in Chapter 12, "The Manger Miracle."

Once a new office location was found and the space built to my needs, I was thrilled to work there. It was beautiful, and best of all, it was bathed in the presence of the Lord. My thoughts of retiring had faded away. Also, the corner office location turned out to be fabulous because the walls of the building were made of glass, and patients could sit in the waiting room and see for miles around. They could watch planes come in and out of airports and see gorgeous sunsets looking westward.

My private office was the premier location with glass walls on two sides. Whenever someone came into that room for the first time, the view would often take their breath away. The truth is that I never planned to have the best view in my private office; it just turned out that way. Even though I had not designed it that way, God had. In all my years of practicing medicine, I had never had an office that compared to that one. God is so good!

About three years later, I was attending the American Academy of Ophthalmology meeting in San Francisco, and as I was walking from one lecture to another, my cell phone rang. It was the practice broker whom I had worked with several years before. Of course, I had not talked to him in a long time because my practice was no longer on the market. He said there was a young doctor who was interested in my practice and wanted to come see it. I was shocked. Now that I was no longer thinking about selling my practice, had God's perfect timing arrived? Was this the consecrated Christian I had requested? With more government changes to medicine looming in the near future, the climate for selling a solo practice of medicine had declined. If this doctor ended up buying my practice, it would surely be by the hand of God.

When he came for a visit, I discovered that he was a serious Christian. He decided to buy the practice, and all the arrangements were made. This was in the fall of 2009. I asked the broker three times to set up a closing date before the end of the year. He said no every time, despite the fact that all the necessary paper work had been done. This puzzled me, because there was no apparent reason for the delay. The closing was scheduled for immediately after the first of the year 2010.

As I reflected on the whole sequence of events, I realized that my practice income had gone up every year after the move to the new facility, and therefore, the value of my practice had increased. It also had greater value because of the beautiful new office. Both of these factors resulted in more revenue than I would have received if my practice had sold a few years earlier in the older office location.

I also noted that if the sale had closed in 2009 as I had wanted, then I would have been in the private practice of medicine for a total of thirty-nine years. But because the broker would not budge from having the closing date in 2010, I had practiced medicine exactly <u>forty years</u>, which is an important recurring number in the affairs of God. This was a miraculous exclamation point to the evidence that God had arranged everything according to His will and in His timing—which is always <u>perfect</u>! I give glory to God for His continual miraculous handling of the affairs of our lives, if we will simply place them in His hands.

From Jerusalem to China

While in Jerusalem in 1979, a stranger invited us to come to a church service at the Church of St. Peter in Gallicantu. I never would have dreamed how that service would impact my life, for there, I met Ruth Ward Heflin, one of the closest friends I have ever had.

We arrived at the service at the appointed time. As we walked in, everyone was at the altar singing and dancing. We stood in a pew, and shortly, someone came to us and invited us to worship with them, which we gladly did. We had never experienced worship like that. Everyone was dancing in lines or circles and singing what I later learned were "new songs." Someone would start singing a phrase that the Holy Spirit had dropped into their heart. It would be simple enough for everyone to sing along. We would sing this song over and over until God gave someone else a "new song." This went on without interruption for about an hour, with no musicians and no apparent leader. Everyone was equally involved.

After this wonderful time of worship, people started going toward the seats. A tall, stately woman came over to me and said, "Don't I know you?" I assured her we had never met. She was someone you would never forget once you had met her. She said that she was sure we had met and said to give her a few minutes to remember where. Then she said she had been in America during the year before and had seen me with Reverend R.W. Schambach on the Phil Donahue Show, verifying the miraculous ability of Ronald Cohen to see without an eye.

"You are an eye doctor," she said. My response was, "I guess you do know me." She asked me to speak the next morning at Mt. Zion Fellowship, which was their ministry in Jerusalem.

Ruth had ministry teams in Los Angeles and Hong Kong that had been waiting for months to get visas to go into China. This was at a time when it was extremely difficult to get a visa to go into China. That night Ruth prayed for the Lord to speak through me the next day and show her what to do about these teams that were getting weary of waiting.

Of course, I knew nothing at all about Ruth's circumstances or her prayer. As I asked the Lord what to speak about, He told me to share the miraculous faith journey we were experiencing in the building of a five-million-watt television station in the Dallas/Ft. Worth Metroplex. The title He gave me was, "Walking on the Water." As soon as I announced the title and began speaking about our walk of faith, Ruth knew exactly what the Lord wanted her to do. She immediately booked the next flight out of Israel to Los Angeles.

This was on the Saturday before Thanksgiving, and the Lord had told her, "On Thanksgiving Day, you will have something to be thankful for." She had to hurry to make it to Hong Kong by Thanksgiving. She also had to put her faith in high gear to believe God for the visas that had so far been impossible to acquire. She had to "Walk on the Water."

By the time she got to Los Angeles, they had received the long-awaited visas. She flew to Hong Kong the next day where they obtained the necessary entry permits. They arrived at their ministry house in Hong Kong just in time to have a wonderful Thanksgiving dinner. Ruth definitely had something to be thankful for on this Thanksgiving Day, just as the Lord had told her.

When you look back at the sequence of events, you realize how perfectly God timed every facet of this experience. 1) He had a stranger invite us to the meeting at the Church of St. Peter in Gallicantu at the very moment Ruth desperately needed to hear from God about China. 2) He had Ruth recognize me from a TV program she had seen the year before, which in itself is a miracle. 3) He had her invite me to speak the next morning. 4) He had me speak on "Walking on the Water," which was the very title that answered her prayer for direction. If she had not gotten that word from God on that very morning, she would not have had time to get to Hong Kong by Thanksgiving because the travel agency in Israel closed at noon on the Sabbath (the day I was speaking). 5) He had all the visas released at the same time Ruth arrived in Los Angeles, which barely gave her enough time to get to Hong Kong and get the entry permits on Thanksgiving Day. We see clearly how God's timing is perfect and how He is in control of every tiny detail if we will just obey Him. What a mighty God we serve!

Dr. Vaughan at the Western Wall
Jerusalem, Israel

Geri and Dr. Vaughan in Jerusalem

The RV Loan

About eleven years ago, at the specific instruction of the Holy Ghost, I bought a very nice RV (motor home) with three "slide outs." I had taken out a loan to buy it and had been making monthly payments faithfully over all these years. While I was practicing medicine, I had never felt the Lord wanted me to pay off that loan, but to just continue making payments every month.

After retiring, I still had the burden of those monthly payments. I made my payments online every month to a certain financial institution. I also had a credit card from the same financial institution, which I also paid online every month. These two payments were listed one above the other in my list of monthly bills since they were both to the same bank.

One month, I had a very large credit card bill because I had been traveling abroad on a ministry trip and had charged everything on that one credit card. When it came time to pay bills, I paid off the entire credit card bill.

A few days later, I discovered that instead of paying the financial institution for the credit card, I had accidentally pushed the line above it on the list of bills and paid that large amount on my RV loan instead. Wow, what a huge mistake. Now I still owed the big credit card bill, and it was too late to retrieve the accidental payment on the RV. All of this was very unlike me because I am usually very meticulous about important things like this.

As I began to reflect on everything that had happened, I wondered if the Lord had had a hand in that "mistake." You know He can sometimes accomplish His perfect will through what we might consider "mistakes." I called the company that had the RV loan and asked them how much I still owed, and how much the interest would be over the period of years that I still needed to pay. I was surprised to find out that I now only owed about the same amount that I had just paid "by accident." Furthermore, the interest payments would be about one thousand dollars a year to continue the loan as it was. God knows my heart. I would never have considered paying off the very large amount I had owed. But now that I only owed half that much and would save a thousand dollars a year in interest by paying off the loan, it seemed like a good idea.

After all the years of being led <u>not</u> to pay off that loan, He now tricked me into doing it. I always think of Romans 8:28 in situations like this. "And we know that all things work together for good to them that love God, to them who are the called according to his purpose." He is a master at taking situations that seem bad and turning them into something good.

I am happy to say that I did pay off the remaining RV loan and am now set free. I can delete that item on my list of monthly bills. His ways are so much higher than ours, and in addition, He is sometimes downright funny.

"Go to China—NOW"

We were flying back from a three week trip to the Middle East when the Lord spoke to me very clearly and said, "Go to China, and do it NOW." I was shocked. Here we were, still in flight from one trip, and He was telling me to immediately go on another trip. Keep in mind that I had a flourishing solo medical practice, and being gone for three weeks meant my desk would be piled high with paper work. There would also be many patients clamoring to come in right away, plus my usual load of surgery and office visits. From my point of view, this would definitely NOT be a good time to leave again.

But the Lord had said to go NOW. So as soon as I got home, I began trying to get us visas to go to China. Since I had never tried to go there before, I had no idea how hard it would be. At that time (December 1980), China had just come out of the Cultural Revolution and the country was still primarily closed to foreigners. Over and over I tried with no success. But I knew that when the Lord says to do something, He will make a way where there seems to be no way. He will open doors that no man can close. Therefore, I scheduled flights to Hong Kong and trusted the Lord to get visas for us when we arrived there. (Hong Kong was still a British territory at that time and not part of China.)

Upon arrival in Hong Kong, I immediately began trying again to get the required visas. After several days, the Chinese government granted them to us and assigned us to an English-speaking group of eight people with a government appointed tour guide. I was obedient to God's command to go, and He was faithful to make a way to get the visas.

Nothing could have prepared us for what we saw and felt in China. It was January 1981 when we finally got there. We were first taken across the border from Hong Kong into Guangzhou. The weather there in southern China was somewhat like Miami, Florida, in the winter. We wore light jackets and walked along the streets with the thousands of Chinese pedestrians. Motor vehicles were very rare to see. Some people had bicycles, but most people were simply walking as their only mode of transportation. The adults, men and women alike, were all dressed uniformly in "Mao" jackets and trousers, mainly blue. Colored attire was only seen on babies and small children.

As we walked through an open market, I stood still and stared at some objects I could not identify. They were small round bundles tied with string, about two to three inches in diameter with various heights—some three inches, some four inches, and some about six inches. They looked like nothing I had ever seen for sale in a food market before. As I stepped a few feet closer, I recognized them as centipedes, some longer than others, neatly tied and ready for consumption. Wow, that was a new food item for me! We also saw skinned cats and dogs in the meat market.

I can't say the things to eat were appealing to us, but on the other hand, the people were wonderful. They were smiling, cheerful, and friendly although we did not speak the same language. Simple things, like having a little pet bird in a cage, seemed to make them very happy. How much we should learn from that! They were extremely honest. You could leave your gold watch or a stack of hundred dollar bills on your night stand. The cleaning crew would dust around them and leave them untouched. The hotel rooms had no locks on the doors.

From Guangzhou, we were flown to Beijing, which is more like Minnesota in the winter. Our luggage was taken to the hotel, and we were taken straight from the airport to a walking tour of the Forbidden City. The wind was blowing a gale, the temperature was freezing, there was no heat anywhere, and our heavy coats were in our suitcases in the hotel. Needless to say, we were frozen and in a miserable state. As we walked along, I asked our Chinese tour guide what faith he believed in. He said, "We believe in ourselves." He asked me what I believed in, and I told him, "I believe in Jesus." His response was, "Who is that?" I was astounded that this educated, bilingual man had never heard of Jesus. They knew about Coca Cola and Mickey Mouse, but they didn't know about Jesus...amazing!

We discovered that most of the hotels in China had no heat. The country was not equipped or prepared for visitors. The water was brown, so every meal was prepared starting with brown water. It was questionable whether bathing in brown water was getting you cleaner or dirtier. Food was apparently in short supply judging by what we were served. Every person in our little tour group got sick. One night, I passed out in the hotel room trying to make it to the bathroom. I am telling you all of this, not to degrade China in any way, but because it is actually the way it was in those days.

Despite all of this, we fell in love with China and her people. The love that God put in our hearts was so strong that it has lasted all of our lives. Why did He tell me so emphatically to go to China at that specific time? I believe it was to let us see the way these Chinese people were—so kind, and honest, and simple in those early years, and to plant seeds of love that would only grow with time. **His timing is perfect**.

Since then, we have returned many times to shed God's love abroad to His Chinese people. My heart was torn on a later trip to realize that many people in China needed eye care and were unable to get it for a variety of reasons. I was so moved by this realization that we later built an eye surgery center in Beijing (Glory Eye Center) where we did much free eye surgery on those that were poor and blind. We even reached out into far western China and far north into Inner Mongolia to do surgery on the needy and help train their eye surgeons.

In Inner Mongolia, I was given a beautiful Mongolian horse with a plaque saying, "To Dr. Elizabeth R. Vaughan—An Ambassador of Light." It was engraved in three languages, Mongolian, Chinese, and English. I cherish it to this day, along with many, many gifts that have been sacrificially given to me over the years by these generous Chinese people.

Mongolian Horse

During the time we spent in China, God supernaturally attracted media attention to the work we were doing. There were magazine, newspaper, and TV reporters around me everywhere. They were clamoring for interviews. One question they commonly asked was, "Why are you doing this?" They couldn't figure out why I would come help their people at my own expense. The answer I always gave was the truth: "God has given me a love for the Chinese people." That told them that there was a God and that He loved the Chinese people. I always wore a jade cross around my neck, even in surgery, which confirmed the source of my love.

Because I always told them of my love for them, their articles and reports would nearly always contain something about love. In fact, CCTV (Central China Television) had a prime-time program about Glory Eye Center and my work in China. That program aired in all parts of China. Someone told me that the people across the country knew me. I didn't believe that until one afternoon when I had a little time off from doing surgery.

I went with Geri to the "silk market," which was comprised of small shops, out of doors, near the American Embassy. Geri was busy looking at Beanie Babies while I stood in the middle of the walkway enjoying the day. The shop keeper that was showing Geri the Beanie Babies saw me standing there. He called out to me in broken English, and said, "You doctor loves Chinese people." I said I was and went over to shake his hand. At that moment in time, the price for Geri's beanies fell dramatically. This event made me realize what God had done, without any effort whatsoever on my part. I believe it was all about laying a ground work for the Gospel of the love of Jesus to flood into China in <u>God's perfect timing</u>.

Geri buying Beanie Babies
near the silk market in Beijing, China

We have watched China change radically over the passing decades. Now, her cities are filled with many, many cars. Modern hotels are available that have not only clean water and comfortable temperatures, but all the amenities offered anywhere in the world. McDonalds and other fast food restaurants are everywhere. Her people dress in whatever colors and styles they prefer. China was wonderful when we first met her, and she is still wonderful today.

I never would have dreamed, flying home from the Middle East when God said "Go to China and do it NOW," that His purpose was to plant our feet in new soil with a love that would last a lifetime.

His thoughts are so much higher than ours, and His ways are beyond reproach. We must learn to heed the words of that old hymn: "Trust and obey, for there's no other way to be happy in Jesus than to <u>trust</u> and <u>obey</u>.

The Condo Miracle

I had a condominium in a lovely high-rise building in Dallas, but after selling my practice of medicine and moving away from Dallas, the condo needed to be sold. After many months of preparation to get it ready to sell, I hired a realtor and put it on the market. I had prayed and asked the Lord to bring in a buyer, so I told the realtor that it would sell quickly, even though the real estate market was very sluggish at the time.

Despite my prayer, months went by and still no buyer came. Every month, I had to pay the substantial homeowner fees, which were due whether I was living there or not. This was a drain on my finances since I had purchased a home elsewhere. I was now obligated to maintain two homes with insurance, taxes, and upkeep. I prayed even more and still stood strong in faith that God would bring in a buyer. It was now obvious that the Lord was not in a hurry about the sale like I was.

One day, I traveled back to Dallas to bring something to the now empty condo and discovered leaking water from the ceiling of the master bathroom. The ceiling had partially fallen down into the room, and the water had totally ruined the imported silk wall covering. The building maintenance man had already gone home for the day, so they called him to come back to the condo. By the time he got there, more water had ruined more things in the room. He examined the situation and declared that he could not handle it, and a plumber would have to be called in to get to the leaking pipe above the ceiling and repair it.

By this time, it was late in the evening, and needless to say, the plumber's fees were higher than the ceiling he was working on! He found that the leak was in a horizontal pipe leading from the main condominium water line into my condo unit. I found out that the condominium bylaws stated that if any leak occurred in a horizontal pipe it was the homeowner's responsibility to repair it, not the building's responsibility. So the costly plumbing repair, ceiling repair, wall repair, and redecorating costs were now added to the monthly condo fees, taxes, insurance, etc.

Put yourself in that circumstance and imagine how it would make you feel. As bad as that situation was, I was very grateful that God had led me to the condo in perfect timing to find the leak early. If I had not found it then, it could have flooded my entire condo and leaked to the neighbors' condo units beneath mine, ruining theirs and causing an enormous nightmare for us all. God is so wonderful to protect His children and order our footsteps.

After eight and a half months of waiting, I had a dream that the condo sold on the 4th or 5th of some month. I didn't know what month, but I had an overwhelming feeling of elation in my dream. I was sooo very happy to no longer have those expensive monthly condo dues any more. When I awoke, the dream had filled me with joy at the prospect of the sale.

God had shown me years ago that it would have been better for Miriam and the women of Israel to dance with their tambourines expecting the Red Sea to be parted, rather than waiting to see it part with their own eyes and then rejoicing. With this lesson in mind, I began to thank the Lord for the sale before I saw a buyer.

About ten days after the dream, the Lord told me the condo would sell "in due time." After getting this word I was completely at ease about the sale. I knew God was in control, and it no longer mattered whether "due time" was a week, a month, a year or ten years. I knew He would supply all my needs, so I totally released it into His hands. The timing was no longer a concern. What peace total release brings!

Ten days later, the broker called and said we had a contract on the condo, and the buyer wanted a quick closing date. Note that after waiting nine months for a buyer, it only took ten days for one to come forth after my total release of the matter into the hands of the Lord. Note also that the word from God changed everything in my heart and mind and enabled the total release.

The title company sent all the paper work concerning the sale to me. I had to sign an affidavit that all the information was correct. I noticed that the year listed as the year I bought the condo was incorrect. I called the title company and told them I did not recall the exact date of the sale, but I knew that the year listed was incorrect. She said that a mistake like that never happened, but she looked up the correct date while I was on the phone with her. She said the date I had signed the papers to buy the condo was actually **4/24/1992**. I thanked her and hung up.

As I studied the papers further, I realized that the date I had signed the papers for the sale of the condo was **4/24/2012, exactly twenty years to the day later.** If the title company had not made the mistake on the original purchase date, I probably would never have noticed God's perfect timing, but because of the mistake, the date was brought to my attention. Only God can coordinate all these intricate details.

Knowing nothing about my dream that the condo would sell on the 4th or 5th of some month, the broker and the title company set the closing date for **5/4/12, exactly** as God had shown me. My rejoicing was very great, and the fact that God has everything under control was very real. There can be no doubt that this is another miracle of **God's perfect timing!**

Chapter 10

More Revelations

Whose Life Is This?

In Acts 1:1-2, Luke writes, "The former treatise (book of Luke) have I made, O Theophilus, of all that Jesus <u>began</u> both to do and teach, Until the day in which he was taken up...." When Jesus was crucified, resurrected, and ascended, why did Luke say that Jesus <u>began</u> to do and say things? How could He continue to do and say things when He was in heaven? Jesus continued to do His works through the Holy Spirit in His followers, as recorded throughout the book of Acts.

Today, Jesus needs people who are willing to let Him continue His works through them. It takes the responsibility of doing the works off of you and places it on Jesus, since they are His works, not yours. Your total responsibility is to "trust and obey" as the old hymn states. He wants us to rest in His arms and enjoy watching Him live His life through us. **Jesus needs a body**.

This leads each of us to an important question. Whose life am I living? Look at it this way. Jesus was born as a baby just like you and me. He learned to crawl, then walk, then learned a work skill just like other people do in life. But whose life was it really? As a man in his thirties, He said:

"I assure you, most solemnly I tell you, the Son is able to do nothing from Himself (of His own accord); but He is able to do only what He sees the Father doing. For whatever the Father does is what the Son does in the same way..." (John 5:19 AMP).

"My meat is to do the will of him that sent me, and to finish his work" (John 4:34).

"He that hath seen me hath seen the Father..." (John 14:9).

Yes, He was living a life on this earth as a human being. But it was really the life of God, His Father, that was being lived through Jesus the Son. Jesus had chosen to lay His life down and let his Father use His life however He chose. Throughout His life and even unto Calvary, Jesus set aside his own will for the Father to have His will. "Not my will, but Thine, be done" (Luke 22:42).

One of the names given Jesus was Emmanuel, which means, "God with us" (Matt. 1:23). Truly his life was the life of God being lived out in front of us to show us the way God wants us to live. In fact, Jesus states clearly, "The Father that dwelleth in me, he doeth the works" (John 14:10). It was God the Father, working through Jesus by the power of the Holy Spirit, that was doing the works. In the natural it was Jesus' life, but in the Spirit, it was the Father's life.

The point I want us to see is that the life of Jesus of Nazareth, the man with his own desires, was laid down willfully so that God could use Jesus to live His life on the earth. The reason for emphasizing this point is because Jesus wants to live His life through us in the same way that His Father lived His life through Jesus. The only way that this can be accomplished is for each of us to lay down our lives (our will) and make it subservient to Jesus in the same way that Jesus did with his Father. In this way, Jesus can live His life and exercise His will through us. **Jesus needs your body**.

We read about this throughout the scriptures, but somehow it doesn't seem to become a reality in the lives of most Christians because they want to "do their own thing" and exert their own will in every circumstance. Jesus taught us to do the opposite. "If any one desires to be my disciple, let him deny himself [disregard, lose sight of and forget himself and his own interests] and take up his cross and follow Me…" (Matt. 16:24 AMP). He also says in Matthew 10:38-39, "He that taketh <u>not</u> his cross, and followeth after me, <u>is not worthy of me</u>. He that findeth his life shall lose it: and he that loseth his life for my sake shall find it." "Losing his life" means surrendering his will.

A beautiful example of this is found in the life of Kathryn Kuhlman, a powerful instrument in God's hand, who is now in heaven. She came to a point in her life where she went to a dead-end street in Portland, Oregon, and died to herself (her own self-will). In other words, she completely gave up what <u>she wanted</u> in her life to embrace what <u>God wanted</u> to do in her life.

After this commitment, God began doing spontaneous healing miracles in her meetings. The meetings turned into huge crusades where thousands would have to stand outside the building because the auditorium was filled to capacity. People would come from all over the world to be healed by God in her meetings.

On one such occasion, she was standing on the stage back in Portland, Oregon. God had just healed a man who had been confined to a wheelchair for years because of debilitating multiple sclerosis. As he now rose from his wheelchair and walked across the stage, people in the auditorium were clapping and cheering at what God had just done before their eyes.

At that moment God said to Miss Kuhlman, "<u>You lost your life for My sake, but you found it in Me</u>." In her heart she realized, "<u>I found my life,</u>

for I lost my will to His will." The life she lost was doing things in the flesh that her will dictated. The life she gained was the life of Christ. The result of obeying Jesus in the act of crucifying one's own will is glorious.

Jesus declared, "Verily, verily, I say unto you, he that believeth on me, the works that I do shall he do also; and greater works than these shall he do; because I go unto my Father" (John 14:12). The fact is that no one can do these "works" (healings, miracles, wonders) but Jesus Himself. He is looking for available vessels that have been emptied of flesh (self-will) that He can do the works through—vessels that are willing to be nothing that Christ can be all. Jesus wants the liberty to say and do His will through us without hindrances, just like the Father did through Jesus as a man. He wants us to be able to truthfully say with Paul, "I am crucified with Christ: nevertheless I live; yet not I, but Christ liveth in me" (Gal. 2:20).

Remember what Jesus told Clarice about raising the dead pastor. **"I can't go over there. Nothing manifests in this dimension without a body. You take Me over there…."** This was a profound revelation to me. It was screaming at me that Jesus needs our bodies, our feet, our mouth, our hands, etc., to do His will through us. Obviously, we cannot do the miracles; Jesus is the only one with that power. But on the other hand, Jesus can't do them either without a yielded, crucified vessel to walk over to the person, lay hands on them, and speak the words as Jesus directs by the Holy Ghost. The accomplishment of God's perfect will requires both Jesus and a crucified human vessel. It is like a joint venture with both parties essential. The only hope for the glory of God to be manifested on this earth is for Christ to be in control in you. "Christ in you, the hope of glory" (Col. 1:27).

Put your hand over your heart right now, and ask yourself, "Whose life is this?" If your honest answer is, "This is my life to live as I please," then you have a decision to make. You can either continue as you are and completely miss God's perfect will for your life—or you can make a quality decision to crucify your self-will, ask Jesus to live His life through you, and enter into a life filled with the glory of the Lord. Make that decision <u>now</u>! Eternity can't wait. **Jesus needs your body!**

God's Timing

Has there ever been a time in your life when you knew God was going to do something and you wanted it to happen <u>right now</u>? In fact, yesterday would have been more to your liking. Well I have learned that no matter how much I want it right now, God's timing is always perfect. His ways are higher than our ways, and His thoughts are higher than our thoughts. Therefore, our timing is flawed and imperfect compared to His. He knows the end from the beginning, and all we know is the beginning.

Think about it like this: If you were baking a cake, and it took one hour to bake it completely, would you remove it from the oven in thirty minutes just because your child begged you to? The child does not know how to bake this cake. He does not realize that the inside would still be mush after thirty minutes. And if you did remove it and serve it to him prematurely, he would not like it at all. He wanted the perfect cake he had in his mind, not the pile of mush you would serve him. He would say, "Why did you give me this gooey mush?" Of course, your only answer would be, "Because you begged for the cake <u>right now</u>, so I let you have it."

This sounds like a ridiculous scenario of the parent doing something very foolish by bending to the desires of the child. Thankfully, God is too wise and loves us too much to be moved by the timing we think is right.

I also think about the Chinese orchids I planted last fall. If they had a mind of their own and were so excited about blooming forth for the glory of God and for my pleasure that they decided to come out of the ground and bloom in January when it was thirty degrees, of course they would die. They would sacrifice their very lives because they were too impatient to wait on God's perfect timing to bloom.

Think also about the crippled man begging at the Gate Beautiful. Several times a week, Peter and John would probably have passed him as they entered the temple. They had probably heard him call out for money hundreds of times in their lives. They had never stopped before and commanded him to rise in the name of Jesus. Why did they do it on that particular day? In fact, why didn't Jesus heal him as he passed him day after day sitting in the same place? There can be only one answer. It was the day of God's perfect timing—as no other day had been. That is the day the Holy Spirit moved on Peter and John to speak healing. We don't know why God chose that particular day, but He had reasons beyond our understanding.

Why did Jesus appear to Paul on the day he was traveling to Damascus? He could have come to him any other day, in any other place. He came at that very moment in time because it was the exact, perfect moment in the plans of the Father. We can't expect to always understand when or why He does things. "Trust in the LORD with all thine heart; and lean not unto thine own understanding. In all thy ways acknowledge him, and he shall direct thy paths" (Prov. 3:5-6). What we do understand is that His ways are impeccable, as no human's could be.

You can think of many other examples of God's perfect timing. Remember Peter falling into a trance on top of the building while waiting for a meal to be prepared and seeing unclean animals come down before him? He was told to go with the men who were at the door. The vision was perfectly coordinated with them knocking at the door. Only God can do this. It is supernatural timing.

Too often, we are impatient to have things done when we want them done, instead of being calm, patient, and satisfied to wait on God's perfect timing. "We do not want you to become lazy, but to imitate those who through faith and patience inherit what has been promised" (Heb. 6:12 NIV). "But they that wait upon the LORD shall renew their strength; they shall mount up with wings as eagles; they shall run, and not be weary; and they shall walk, and not faint" (Isa. 40:31).

Sometimes I will watch the little sparrows sitting on a small branch swaying forward and backward as the wind blows the branch. They seem content, even if they are being blown about. They are not stressed or fretful. They are patiently sitting there waiting for the right moment to fly to another perch. It would be good for us to emulate the birds and "be anxious for nothing" as God advised (Phil. 4:6). God takes care of them, and He will take care of us too—if we are not in such a hurry that we fly off of our perch prematurely and lose the blessing.

The Poker Chips

There are times in life when things can be very difficult, but God has a wonderful way of making good come out of them (Rom. 8:28). February 2015 was the beginning of one of those times. Here is some of the background on this episode.

Geri, my long time ministry team partner, had gone into kidney failure in 2001 and was forced to go on kidney dialysis to save her life. Her father had died from kidney failure when Geri was a young child. Her daughter had died of kidney failure when she was a young adult. Now, it was Geri's turn to fight the same battle.

We had been traveling the nations and ministering in the name of Jesus together for many years. And since she had no family left, I stepped into the role of caring for her during this health crisis. Neither of us had any idea what long, tumultuous times lay ahead with her health issues.

I will save the miracle of her kidney transplant for another time. We thought the transplant would be the final answer to her health problems, but it was just the beginning. The years that followed were filled with hospitalizations over and over with uncontrolled urinary tract infections. Some of these were imminently life-threatening since the infection had gotten into her blood stream. Many other complications arose as side effects from the anti-rejection medications that she had to take as a transplant patient.

Let's fast forward to February 27, 2015, a freezing day with ice on the roads. Despite being on continual antibiotics every day of her life, Geri had spiked a high fever during the night, which meant she must get to the hospital as fast as possible before the bacteria could get into her blood stream again. She was so weak that I called neighbors to help me get her into the car. All three of us pushed and shoved with all our might, but we could not lift her listless body into the car. So with her body half in and half out of the car, I reached into my pocket and called 911. The fire department came, and two young, strong men literally lifted her into the car. We were thankful to finally be on our way to the hospital in Dallas, even though the roads were covered with ice.

Of course they admitted her immediately and started IV antibiotics. After about a week, the infection was under control, but she was too weak to go home, so she was sent to a rehab center. They worked on getting her stronger, and after two weeks of therapy, she finally got to go home. She was so happy to be home, and so were her dogs.

She was still on antibiotics when she spiked another high fever only five days after coming home. Again, I rushed her back to Dallas—this time in the middle of the night, and again they admitted her to the hospital. The doctors were stunned and puzzled by this quick recurrence of another uncontrolled infection. What in the world was going on in her body to cause this? The infectious disease specialist (we believe, led by the Holy Ghost) ordered a CT scan of the abdomen. To everyone's surprise, it showed a big abscess from the colon, which had caused a fistula into the bladder. No wonder she was having so much trouble with recurrent urinary tract infections! This was not a situation compatible with life.

Needless to say, she needed abdominal surgery as soon as feasible. She was so weak with so much infection in her body, that they spent many days trying to get her ready for the surgery. Finally, they decided they had to operate despite her debilitated condition. The surgery date was set for the day after Easter. Mary, our longtime friend from Oklahoma, drove down to Dallas on Easter Sunday to be with us for this big surgery on Monday.

By the time the surgery was finished on Monday, and Geri was taken to ICU from the recovery room, it was night time. During all the weeks Geri had been in the hospital and rehab, I had stayed with her day and night. I can't remember a single night when we had gotten much sleep at all. Geri was ill and very restless, which kept us both awake, in addition to the hospital and rehab staff interrupting the little sleep we could have gotten with a continual parade of things they had to do for her. Of course, Mary had gotten no sleep either the one night before surgery that she spent in the hospital room with us. So Mary was tired, and I was exhausted by the time Geri was settled in ICU.

We decided to go to Geri's hospital room and try to get some rest. We turned the lights out at about eleven p.m. At two a.m., a nurse came through the door, turned on the lights, and abruptly said, "You have to get out of this room, right now. We have to clean it for other patients." Mary and I were shocked. We had assumed Geri would retain her same hospital room after surgery. Apparently we were mistaken, so at two a.m., we got up and began packing things.

You know how it is when you are in the same room for a prolonged time; you accumulate things. Every possible space in that room was full of those "accumulations." It took us about an hour and a half, with both of us working as hard as we could, to get all our things packed. We borrowed carts to carry everything down to the lobby of the hospital where we loaded it all into Mary's SUV. She then took me to the parking garage, and we loaded all Geri's things and my things into my little Chevy Malibu. Mary decided to drive back to Oklahoma in the middle of the night since we had nowhere to stay. I thanked her profusely for coming down to be with us, hugged her goodbye, and off she went into the night.

I was now alone in the back seat of the Malibu. The front passenger seat was full, the trunk was full, the back floorboard was full, and most of the back seat was full. The car was loaded to its fullest capacity. I tried to lie down in the remaining tiny space in the back seat. There were Easter lilies Geri had received from two different friends, plus some spring flowers all on the back floorboard. They were tall enough to be right in my face when I tried to lie down. What better time or place could there be to pray than here in this tiny space, with an exhausted body, flowers in my face, and nowhere to stay for some unknown future period of time? This was a perfect circumstance to be alone with God!

I asked Him to "swallow me up." He said He couldn't do that until I was empty. He showed me a vision of a poker table with a pile of chips in front of me. I then saw myself pushing the stack of chips from my side of the table to His. What was previously mine now became the property of the Lord. I understood that each chip was some facet of my life that needed to be turned completely over to Him. I made a list of every "chip" that I could think of—my physical and spiritual life, Geri's physical and spiritual life, the ministry He had called us to, the lives of my friends and family members, finances, etc. I even listed things like my home, my cars, my dogs, and my rose bushes, all of which had been sorely neglected all spring because I had not been at home to take care of them. The bottom line is that I gave everything in my life to Jesus! I thought I had done this in years gone by, but He had shown it to me in a new, more graphic way. Jesus is so wonderful at making things simple that can seem so complicated.

How liberating that poker chip vision had been. Now, if I ever thought of Geri's well-being, I was instantly reminded that Jesus owned that. If I thought of my pitiful looking rose bushes, again I was reminded that they were not my rose bushes anymore because I had given them to Jesus. He was now the One who owned them and would take care of them. He assured me that the roots were healthy despite the way the branches looked, and He would make the bushes flourish again.

I don't want you to misunderstand and think I would do nothing for the roses just because I no longer owned them. I would still care for them in a prudent way like any gardener, but the ultimate outcome was not my responsibility, it was His. I was simply His designated caretaker, but He was the Owner.

Every situation that now arises in my life is not mine to figure out a solution for because I don't own that chip or any chip. I am "chipless," and I like it that way. That poker example made me not only "chipless," but also "weightless" because the weight of responsibility for all things in life was now squarely on the shoulders of Jesus. My only job is to trust Him and obey Him. That brings peace and joy into my heart and sets me free.

Why don't you shove all your chips over to Jesus also, and join me in a carefree, "chipless" life. "Come unto me, all ye that labour and are heavy laden, and I will give you rest. Take my yoke upon you, and learn of me; for I am meek and lowly in heart: and ye shall find rest unto your souls. For my yoke is easy, and my burden is light" (Matt. 11:28-30). I am sure you can see how a "chipless" life would change everything.

Since the day I wrote all of the above, I have discovered that life keeps dealing me more chips. On two occasions, I have had new circumstances that put unrest in my heart. At first, I would think about the situation and be concerned about it. Then I came to my spiritual senses and realized that this was just another opportunity to give that situation (that chip) to Jesus and trust Him to take care of every tiny detail of the situation. You know there is nothing too big for Him. He has a way of arranging a perfect solution to something that you cannot figure out what to do about.

If you will truly trust Him with it and shove the chip into His hands, then you don't have to worry about it anymore because it is no longer your chip. It belongs solely to Him, and He is not only well able to handle it, He is delighted that you gave it to Him. He does not want His precious children to carry burdens or worries. In fact, God clearly tells us, "Be careful (anxious) for nothing; but in every thing by prayer and supplication with thanksgiving let your requests be made known unto God. And the peace of God, which passeth all understanding, shall keep your hearts and minds through Christ Jesus" (Phil. 4:6-7).

So after two further "chip" circumstances in my life, I am now becoming accustomed to giving every chip to Jesus much faster, so I can actually remain "chipless" every day. That is a win-win situation for both Jesus and me. It is a win situation for Jesus because it keeps this vessel free of clutter that could hinder the flow of His anointing. It is a win situation for me because I stay free and full of peace. Thank God He likes poker chips!

The Vessel

We all begin as a lump of clay, which our Creator molds into a vessel that will be useful to Him and beautiful in His sight. However, He has given us all a free will, which often takes us down a path of polluting our vessel and ending up with it marred and not fit for His use or not reflecting His glory as first intended. At some point in life, if we are wise, we will give our marred vessel into His hands once again and tell Him we are sorry for polluting it. We will ask His forgiveness (repent) and give whatever is left of our lives to Jesus. He is so very, very happy to have your vessel, now yielded and back in His hands. He has the ability to clean it up inside and out for use as He desires. That vessel must be emptied of self and all the filth that self-will brings. This emptying process may take many years and often is never completely accomplished. Paul came as close to this as any person besides Jesus. He declared it this way, "I am crucified with Christ; and it is no longer I who live, but Christ lives in me…" (Gal. 2:20 NASB).

Once the vessel is empty of self, it can be filled with the precious, pure, holy oil of the Holy Spirit—the very life of Christ. Then the oil can be poured out to a dying world with healings, deliverances, and any miracle that is called for. Oil cannot be poured out of a vessel unless oil is in the vessel. If the vessel is filled with dirt, only dirt can be poured out. If it is filled with milk, only milk can be poured out. You can't give out something you do not have, so our goal should be to be filled to overflowing with the same Holy Ghost that filled Jesus.

Jesus wants to pour Himself out to people of every nationality, color, and religious belief. He wants to meet the deepest needs of people's hearts. The only way He can be poured out is if you and I are willing to be crucified to self-will and let Him fill us with Himself. Then our hands become His hands; our mouths becomes His mouth—and so the life of Christ contin-ues on this earth. **All Jesus needs is a body.**

Chapter 11

More Experiences

Geri Is Going Home

On Tuesday, June 7, 2016, Geri spiked a high fever as she had done so many times in the past from urinary tract infections. The nephrologist had told her that she needed to head to the nearest emergency room when this happened. She was also extremely lethargic, not even lifting her head to talk to the organ technician who came to work on her brand new organ. She had been so excited to get it, and now her head hung down, and she said not a word. I told her that I was taking her to Baylor Hospital in Dallas, NOW. She protested, but I had to do what I knew was right for her. As we were rolling out the front door, she began vomiting and required a trash can be taken in the car for the drive to the hospital. She was a sick cookie indeed.

Of course, they admitted her right away and started her on IV antibiotics. After one week, the infection seemed to be under good control, but her kidney function started to deteriorate. The doctors began feverishly doing tests—a kidney biopsy, cat scans of her abdomen and pelvis, a sonogram of her kidney, etc. None of the tests gave any indication about how to stop the decline in kidney function. She had had a kidney transplant in 2002, which had served her well for fourteen years, but now it was faltering.

After two weeks in the hospital, they sent her to a rehabilitation facility. Physical therapy was initiated; however, she was growing weaker day by day instead of getting stronger. Her kidney function continued to decline. I was staying with her 24 hours a day throughout all of this, as I always did. I was very strong in faith, believing that God would raise her up no matter what her kidney did. I was reading healing scriptures day and night and trying to persuade Geri to listen to CDs that would strengthen her faith. She had very little interest in doing anything because she felt so bad.

One day, the Lord gave me three words, "spring forth speedily." I looked them up and discovered that those three words occurred in that sequence in only one place in the word of God. Isaiah 58:8 says, **"your health shall spring forth speedily."** He also gave me a vision with the scripture. I saw a rose bush with 3 or 4 pink roses on it. Very quickly, like overnight, it was completely covered with pink roses on every inch of the bush. This made me even more sure that God was going to raise Geri up, and her health would spring forth speedily. She would be like the rose bush that was supernaturally covered with blossoms very, very quickly. My heart leapt with joy at the prospect.

Finally, the rehab doctor sat down with Geri, looked her straight in the eyes, and told her that he would not recommend dialysis. It might keep her alive a little while longer or she might die during the process. He suggested that she go home on hospice and enjoy her dogs during the few days she had left. She had been saying for days that she wanted to go home, so that is what she decided to do.

Actually, that virtual sentence of death did not hinder my faith because I believed so strongly that God would raise her up. He had told us so many things that He planned to do through us. He had given us very specific dreams and shown us places He would send us and nations He would influence through us. These plans had been corroborated through very reliable prophets of God. As we left the rehab facility, I boldly told them that we would be back to see them when God raised Geri up. I told the staff at the nephrologists' office the same thing, and I believed it with all my heart.

When we got home I lifted each dog into her lap, but she was too weak to pet them. The hospice people were so helpful to us. They brought a Hoya lift to lift her out of bed into a chair in the mornings and then back into bed at night. Geri didn't talk. She had not eaten anything in ten days. She could barely take fluids through a straw. She then became too weak to suck through a straw. The Lord gave me the idea of giving her fluids with a 3cc syringe without the needle. I would give her 1.5cc at a time, and make sure she could swallow it before I gave her any more.

Day and night she would ask for water, and I would gladly give it to her. It was the last strand to life that she had. The only word she could speak was "water," and even then, I knew what she meant whether she could say the word or not. By late morning on Friday, July 22, 2016, she was not able to swallow at all. I did not know if God was going to raise her up while she still had breath or if He would take her for a visit to heaven and send her back, but I still believed He would make a miracle witness out of her one way or the other.

On Saturday morning, July 23, 2016, Geri's lifetime friend, Linda, arrived from Austin. Another friend was with Geri also. I told them I would take a quick shower since they were both there and would be back right away. I had not yet gotten into the shower when one of the women came running to me saying Geri had stopped breathing. I ran as fast as I could to her side. She was gone! I looked at the very accurate time on my cell phone, and it was 12:00 noon <u>exactly</u>. Who can do that but God?

I called some powerful people in God to come and pray with me for God to raise her up. I still believed she would come back to life to bring glory to Jesus Christ for His resurrection power. We prayed for hours, and nothing happened.

After the friends were all gone, the funeral home picked up Geri's body at midnight. That night the Lord told me Geri was not coming back. I was very confused. I asked Him why He had shown us all of those plans if He was going to take her home. His answer was liberating. He said, "She was crying out to Me day and night to take her home, and **My mercy overruled My plans**."

Now I understood. She had been in so much pain for so long. She once told me that if she could only have one day without pain it would be so wonderful. She was having a continual parade of symptoms from different parts of her body. So much of her body was failing—her eyes, ears, feet, legs, hands, arms, shoulders, back, urinary tract, gastrointestinal system, pancreas, neurological system, and on and on. In fact, I had been taking her to twenty-one specialists at the time she went to heaven. I believe that when her kidney failed in addition to everything else, she just wanted out of that agonizing body. She wanted to be with Jesus.

I understood that and was glad that all her pain was gone at last. Instead of being in a wheelchair, she could now run on legs like she did when she was a tennis champion in Dallas at age sixteen. I was still faced with having no ministry partner after forty-two years of traveling the nations with Geri, in the name of Jesus.

The next day was Sunday, and I felt like the Lord was going to speak to me in church. During the song service, I was standing with my eyes closed, worshipping God. I felt someone touch my right shoulder. It was Betsy, the head of the church's prayer ministry, standing beside me. She said she had something for me from God. He had shown her "**two big, gold doors swinging open and you walking through with 'power' and 'strength,'** and you were smiling." What a wonderful, uplifting word from God!

Later in the service, God said to me, **"You have a new partner today…
it's Me."** What a glorious surprise! That revelation totally changed my life.
Jesus was now my partner with no distraction whatsoever. We would go
where He wanted to go, do what He wanted to do, say what He wanted to
say. He was the One in charge of everything, and all I had to do was obey
Him. What an easy, glorious life He had now given me.

God said, "Jesus Christ the same yesterday, and today, and for ever"
(Heb. 13:8). Therefore, I anticipated that He would be doing now what He
had done when He walked the earth as a man. I looked forward with great
anticipation to being able to watch Him heal people and do miracles as He
had always done.

I was still wondering why He gave me the words, "spring forth speedily"
and shown me the vision of the quickly blooming pink rose bush. I asked
Him why He told me this about Geri's health and then took her home. His
answer shocked me. **"That wasn't for Geri. It was for <u>you</u>."**

I never dreamed that it was for me when Geri was the one needing her
health to spring forth speedily. But in the days immediately after she went
home, God made me "spring forth speedily" in ministry. I had to discipline
my thinking, refusing to dwell on what was past, but instead focusing on
what lay ahead. My pastor said, "God has given Dr. Vaughan supernatural
grace." I agree with him, and thank God profusely for it.

During the weeks that followed, the excitement over starting a revival
in Justin, Texas, exploded. A family had been vigorously praying for revival
continuously for over eighty years, and they felt like God's timing was now,
and God's place was Justin. They wanted me to be the speaker in the revival
team. What a thrill to be able to help bring people into the kingdom of
God and to watch God set them free and heal them. A start date was set
for October 2016.

In praying for the location of God's choice, one place under consider-
ation was a wedding chapel in Justin called The Abbey. I decided to stop
by there and see what it looked like. As I walked around and prayed in the

sanctuary, I suddenly noticed that there were bunches of pink roses everywhere in that room. Even the windowsills had pink rose petals scattered all over them. God reminded me of the rose bush that was quickly covered with pink roses, and I felt it was confirmation that The Abbey was the location God had chosen for the revival.

On the next Sunday, there was a young evangelist preaching in the Sunday evening service. After thoroughly expounding on his text, he finished by saying something totally unrelated to his sermon. He said, "See your health spring forth. You can see **health spring forth speedily** in your life." I was amazed, as the Lord was saying the same words He had given me, and totally out of context with anything else that the preacher had said. He then told anyone who felt an anointing to step into the aisle, which I did. He came to me and prophesy came forth. "The anointing is making up the difference. It's going to come on you mightily, and you're going to do what you couldn't have done otherwise in **boldness and authority**. **Big doors are open**…in the name of Jesus." Again the Lord was confirming the word He had given me the week before about doors opening and me going through them with power and authority.

That same night, Joe and Becky Cruse, a music ministry team that had provided music at Geri's funeral, were ministering at our church. After the service, I went to Becky to thank her. Before I could say a word, she said that the Holy Spirit had told her during Geri's funeral that He was not through with me yet, and more international ministry was ahead for me. He said that He would "**open doors for you**," especially in Asia, but also in "other regions." She said that she and Joe had talked about it and felt led to invite me to go to Thailand with them. Immediately the Lord told me to go.

I had been to 47 nations, but Thailand was not one of them. I was amazed that the Lord was sending me through the doors so fast. One week after that, on August 9th, I got a text message from a former employee who is a woman of God. She said she had a word from God for me. "**The gates are open.** You will see places you have been to before, and there are new places ahead. God has ordained you to hit the mark." That was the fourth time in two and a half weeks that God had said to me that the doors or gates were open. I get the point, Lord!

This has been a win-win situation for Geri and for me. She is in heaven, set free from the agony of her failing body. And I'm sure she is playing the biggest pipe organ in heaven, which was always her dream. On the other hand, I am partnered with the King of Kings and the Lord of Lords, and we are on course for the most exciting life imaginable with Jesus Christ in control of this body of flesh. Hallelujah!

Unity

As I was flying back from Boston in 2011, I had brought my good friend Ruth Ward Heflin's book, *Unifying Glory*, along with me to read on the plane. As I was reading it, the young Chinese man sitting next to me commented on what an interesting title the book had. He began to ask me questions about it. I am always delighted to talk about Jesus and His word at any time, in any place. That is my favorite subject by far. So we began a conversation that lasted about three hours, until we arrived at our destination.

I began to tell him how, at the end of His earthly ministry, Jesus had prayed that we would all be one. "Neither pray I for these alone, but for them also which shall believe on me through their word; That they all may be **one**; as thou, Father, art in me, and I in thee, that they also may be **one** in us: that the world may believe that thou hast sent me. And the glory which thou gavest me I have given them; that they may be **one**, even as we are **one**: I in them, and thou in me, that they may be made perfect in **one**; and that the world may know that thou hast sent me, and hast loved them, as thou hast loved me" (John 17:20-23).

Jesus had used the word "ONE" five times in this prayer. Following this, He went straight to Calvary. We can assume from this that unity between the Father, the Son, the Holy Ghost, and <u>us</u> is <u>extremely</u> important in accomplishing God's will on this earth.

He said that he had been studying that passage and was desiring unity. He and a few others had just started a new church the month before our conversation. They felt the need to have a Spirit-filled, Chinese church in their area. The group had grown, however, there was dissention among the members. He and his wife had been working so hard and struggling so much. His wife led praise and worship at church. She spent hours and hours trying to prepare the words to the songs. They were both exhausted.

I spent much time ministering to him, which he put into his computer as we talked. I explained that it all had to be done by the Spirit (not flesh) or it would never grow or change lives. If we can learn to flow with the Spirit in our services and in our lives, then we can see lives changed, and life will be much easier.

The Spirit knows the right way to do everything. What He is looking for is yielded bodies to work through. If his wife can teach the congregation to praise God in the Spirit and worship Him with their whole hearts as they sing, then they can enter His glory realm—where there is peace and hearts are changed. This will also help to bring about unity, because when people are in the Spirit, differences seem to fade away, and love flows instead. I shared with him how God had told me that my responsibility as a minister was: 1) to show up, 2) to be led of the Spirit, and 3) to be full of His word. He would do the rest. I had learned from Ruth that there is an ease in the glory, and that is where we want to live.

In doing cataract surgery, there was a technique called "divide and conquer." The cloudy lens of the eye (which is called a cataract) would be divided. The smaller pieces could then be removed much more easily than if the cataract was left in one big piece. I see Satan using this technique in the world around us today—with people groups hating and killing one another even within the same nation, which ideally should be unified. If he can divide people, it is much easier to get the whole nation in turmoil and conquer it with his wicked ways.

What we need to do as individuals and as nations is to turn our hearts to our Father, God Almighty. If we would allow His love to fill our hearts by His Spirit, then forgiveness and unity would follow. I am convinced that the only way for us to "be made perfect in <u>one</u>," as Jesus prayed, is for the Holy Spirit to sweep across our hearts and our nations with His unifying presence. That is our only hope of being made **one** with Jesus and our Father.

"Buy a Cadillac"

As a child, I had been taken to church every time the doors opened, and I am thankful for that. But going to church does not make a person consecrated. That must be a personal decision from your heart.

As a young adult, I made that decision, and I gave my life to Jesus to use however He chose. I also started studying the Bible vigorously and was very excited about it. I was even memorizing scripture and trying my best to walk in it. But I was about to have a real-life experience that would demonstrate how powerful God's word is.

About this time, there was a big Christian convention in Dallas, and a group of us were going together to the meeting in my car. It was an Oldsmobile convertible, which I had been driving for a number of years and enjoying very much. It had never given me one minute's trouble. One of the ladies riding with me commented on what a nice car it was. I told her that it was getting older and would probably start having problems soon.

After I said that, I had a bad feeling inside of me and wished I hadn't said it, but I didn't know what to do about it in the Spirit. (Now, I would <u>never</u> say anything like that in the first place, but if anything contrary to the word ever did come out of my mouth, I would bind it and cast it away from me immediately, in the name of Jesus.) If you don't realize what power your words have, just listen to what happened to my car.

Not long after that, a parade of things started going wrong with my wonderful car. I was spending so much time and money on repairs that I thought it would be prudent to get rid of it. That HUGE lesson taught me to keep my mouth tightly shut concerning negative things. I had spoken that dilemma onto myself with my words.

God tells us we will have whatever we say (Mark 11:23). He also tells us, "Death and life are in the power of the tongue..." (Prov. 18:21). My experience was living proof of the validity of those scriptures. I certainly got what I said! And my car certainly died. Thank God, it was just a car and not a child or a person or for that matter, any living thing.

I now had another dilemma—I needed a car. I asked the Lord what to do, and much to my surprise, He told me to buy a Cadillac. My dad always thought a Cadillac was the best car on the road, but he had never owned one, and neither had I.

In obedience to the instruction of the Lord, I went down to the Cadillac dealership to look at cars. The salesman asked me what kind I wanted. I was so naive and so ignorant about Cadillacs that I simply told him I wanted one with soft seats. Can you imagine that!

I'm sure every Cadillac that was made had soft seats, but that is what I told him. Instead of laughing in my face, he said he had just the right one for me that had real soft seats. He showed me a brand new white Cadillac Biarritz with white leather interior. It had red pin stripes down the side and red piping on the seats. It was beautiful, and it did have very soft seats. I told him that one would be fine, and I bought it, obligating myself for several years of payments. Wait till you hear what happened next.

Two or three weeks after that, we had an international ministry trip planned. I let my pastor, Reverend Marvin Crow, drive my brand new Cadillac while I was gone. Almost immediately after I came home from the trip, the Lord said to give the car to him. I will always obey God no matter what He says. So I called him and told him I wanted to give him something, and I asked if he would stay in his office later than usual that evening and wait for me. I needed to finish seeing patients and then drive to the church. He did not know what I was bringing, but he said he would wait for me.

When I got there, I walked into his office, dropped the keys on his desk, and told him the car was his. He objected, but I told him he would have to take it up with God because that is what He told me to do. I turned and walked out the door.

Now, I had a dilemma again. For the third time, I still needed a car. Again I asked the Lord what to do, and He told me to buy another Cadillac. God sure must like Cadillacs! This time I knew which one had the softest seats. When I arrived at the dealership this time, they had a baby blue (that is my favorite color) Biarritz elevated on display. If you thought the last car was beautiful, you should have seen this one. It was more sporty than the white one, with mag wheels and a T-top. I immediately fell in love with that car and bought it.

A few days later, I asked Geri to take me to the dealership to pick up my new car. She asked if she could drive it when we left, and I told her she could. We drove a few blocks with me following her as she cheerfully drove my new car.

Suddenly she pulled off the road and started honking the horn and hollering. I had no idea what had happened. I jumped out of the car I was in and ran to my new car with Geri in the driver's seat. I asked her what all the noise was about. She was bouncing up and down on my new soft seat yelling, "The Lord just told me this one was mine." Geri NEVER said the Lord told her something unless He really did, so I knew she was not joking. God had just given my second new Cadillac to Geri.

I got back into the older car and continued following her in what was now her new Cadillac. I now had monthly payments for years on two new Cadillacs, and neither one was mine. As I drove, I told the Lord that for the rest of my life, I did not care what kind of car I was driving as long as it worked well…and I meant it. This whole sequence was started by my words about my Oldsmobile. Have you heard the expression, "Loose lips sink ships?" Well, my loose lips had sunk my Oldsmobile, but believe me that would NEVER happen again. I had learned a lesson that would remain very strong inside of me all the rest of my life. I hope this little story has helped you too.

I might add that cars never meant that much to me after this experience. God has led me to give away many cars over the years, including three Lincolns, four new Cadillacs, one Oldsmobile, two Rolls Royces, and most recently, a beautiful red Hummer. I only do this as the Lord leads, and I am always happy to obey Him. I possessed those cars, but they did not possess me.

Perceive, Believe, and Receive

I want to tell you two true stories about being set free and not being aware of it. The first story was told to me by a man who was a bit mischievous when he was a young boy in the 1950s.

One day, his dad took him along to run some errands. As the father was talking to a shop keeper, the little boy wandered around looking at everything. He ran across a chicken that was very much alive, but its feet were tied, so it could not move. Apparently, the shop keeper's desire was to sell it to someone who wanted the freshest possible chicken dinner. The little boy took his pocket knife and cut the strings that were tied around the chicken's feet.

The chicken did not realize that its bonds had been broken, so it continued to lay there in a horizontal position with its feet together, not moving. This response was good for the shop keeper, who retained the immobile chicken. But it was very bad for the chicken, which probably ended up on someone's dinner table that night.

The second story was told to me by my previous pastor, Reverend Marvin Crow, who had a large family consisting of several boys and one girl. While the pastor was studying, the boys kept running in and out of the house so many times that he finally got up and latched the screen door to lock it shut. The boys, still wanting to run in and out, would come up to the door and hit it. When they tried to open the door they could not get in, so they would run off and play some more.

In a little while, they would run up to the door again, hit it again, but still were unable to open it. This happened over and over. Finally, one of the boys came back up to the door and hit it as usual, at which time the latch flew open. He had been so used to the door being locked that he did not even try to open it. He just ran back out into the yard and started playing again with no perception that he could have walked right into the house.

In both instances, a release had been accomplished, but not perceived. The chicken and the boys suffered the consequences of their lack of perception. Sometimes, we as Christians are guilty of the same lack, and we too suffer the consequences.

An example comes to my mind of a friend who called me one morning crying. She had been having severe difficulty with part of her body. A minister had prayed for her the night before, releasing his faith that God would heal her. She was crying because she was still having the same symptoms the next morning, and therefore believed that she had not been healed. The person desiring healing needs to have faith in what God says about their healing and believe God more than they believe their symptoms. Symptoms change, but God's word is always the same. The Bible is the rock they stand on, and it says, "For we walk by faith, not by sight" (2 Cor. 5:7). Jesus said, "According to your faith be it unto you" (Matt. 9:29). He did not say, "According to your feelings be it unto you." Too much of the time, people walk by what their five senses are telling them instead of what God says.

In Isaiah 53:5, God says, "…with His stripes we are healed." By "stripes," He is referring to the extreme beating Jesus took for us at Calvary. God also says in 1 Peter 2:24, "by whose stripes ye were healed." There can be no mistake from these scriptures that God wants us healed and has made provision for it through Jesus.

We need to perceive (realize, understand) that if God says it and we believe it, then that settles it. What your body is indicating has no relevance on the truth of God's word. If you don't perceive that you are already healed, then you won't be. You will be like the chicken that was no longer bound but didn't realize it.

If you do perceive (realize, understand) that you are healed by Jesus' stripes, then you will believe it in your heart, speak it with your mouth, and it will bring about a manifestation, either immediately or in due time. "For with the heart man believeth unto righteousness; and with the mouth confession is made unto salvation" (Rom. 10:10). This is God's formula for receiving healing as well as salvation. They were both bought for us at Calvary. Perceive, believe, and receive.

How does a person get saved? First, he must realize that God loves us and is not willing that anyone perish, meaning go to hell (2 Pet. 3:9). He loved us so much that He was willing to send His only Son, Jesus Christ the Messiah, to take our sins on Himself, shed His blood, and die for our sins.

If a person will perceive these truths and repent (i.e. tell God they are sorry for the wrongs they have done, and make an about face, turning away from their sin), then they will be saved. At this point, the person must perceive that the door to heaven is open to them, and they are free to enter into God's house. This perception should bring great relief and joy. Don't be like Pastor Crow's boys who had an open door to enter in, but they did not perceive it, therefore, they did not enter into the house. Perceive, believe, and receive.

Dealing with attacks from hell is another area where perception (realizing, understanding) is critical. "And having spoiled principalities and powers, he made a show of them openly, triumphing over them in it (the cross)" (Col. 2:15). So Jesus defeated Satan and all his imps from hell. Then God "raised him from the dead, and set him at his own right hand in the heavenly places, Far above all principality, and power, and might, and dominion, and every name that is named, not only in this world, but also in that which is to come: And hath put all things under his feet" (Eph. 1:20-22).

Now here is another critical part of this that we need to understand. We are seated with Christ, which means that we too are far above all principality and power, and might and dominion, and every name that is named (Eph. 2:4-6). So if the enemy tries to attack you with sickness, fear, depression, guilt for past sins that are already erased by the blood of Jesus or any other vile things from hell, then this should be your response: Remind him that you are seated with Jesus far above him in heavenly places, and therefore, you have total and absolute authority over him in the name of Jesus. You rebuke him, bind him, and kick him out of your thoughts and out of your life. He has to obey because of the name of Jesus. You are standing in His stead (2 Cor. 5:20).

The devil would like to make you think he has power over you, and you are bound like the chicken with his feet tied. But the truth is that you are set free by the blood of the Lamb and the word of your testimony. There are no strands around your feet. You, like the chicken, can stand up and be "free as a bird." (Pardon the pun.) All you have to do is perceive it, believe it, and receive it.

Costa Rica

Our first trip to Costa Rica was at the invitation of an evangelist friend and his wife. They had been working in Costa Rica for several years and wanted us to come down and hold meetings at various places around the nation. They would arrange everything. We were delighted to go and share Jesus. Several events stand out in my mind about this trip.

One night, we were invited to hold a meeting in the upstairs of an older building. The people were on fire for God. Toward the end of the service, I invited anyone who needed healing to come forward. There was a long line of people across the altar that we prayed for. One man was memorable. He had an eye patch over one eye. Not knowing what had happened to him, I prayed for God to heal his eye. I then proceeded to tear off the bandage and drop it to the ground.

In total amazement, he started jumping up and down, shouting that his vision was now perfect and his eye no longer had the pain it had had moments before. He then told about how acid splashed in his eye that day while at work. The eye doctor had seen him and bandaged the eye, telling him not to remove the bandage. His vision was severely impaired in the injured eye. His wife came running up to the altar and grabbed the eye patch, which was now on the floor under my foot. I guess she thought he might need it again, but he didn't. "If the Son therefore shall make you free, ye shall be free indeed" (John 8:36).

As an eye surgeon, I knew how severely damaging acid in the eye usually is. It can often lead to permanent blindness. Of course, God can and does heal impossible health problems. The worse the circumstance, the bigger miracle it is, and the more glory goes to Him.

On a day we had off, our friend took us to a rain forest where I had really wanted to see the macaws in their native habitat. Little did I know that these birds stayed in the very top of some very tall trees. I discovered this after we walked in mud in the rain (hence the name rain forest) for a long way. He finally stopped and pointed upward to show me where the birds were. I could barely see them, they were so far away in the top of the trees. I actually needed binoculars, which I did not have. I may not have been able to experience seeing the birds like I wanted to, but I certainly did get to experience a rain forest first hand.

Another wonderful experience was taking a boat trip down small rivers in the jungle, where we saw beautiful, large blue butterflies and slow sloths climbing in the trees with almost imperceptible movement. Monkeys were yelling at us from the trees and jumping around vigorously. We were in their domain, and they did not like it. It was raining that day, but still it was one of the best days of my life, spent in nature with God's amazing creatures.

Prior to our second trip to Costa Rica, we had been traveling in several countries and were a bit road weary, so I promised Geri three days of relaxation before we started a crusade there. Geri loved to fish and considered it relaxing. So I called the pastor who was sponsoring the crusade and asked if he knew of a lovely place where we could rest and fish before the meetings started. He immediately said he knew of the perfect place for that. It was a beautiful resort in the mountains with a lake nearby for fishing and a warm pool of water where you could relax and see the stars at night. That sounded great, so I asked him to book it for us. Finally, we could prop our feet up and rest!

When we arrived in Costa Rica, he had arranged for his secretary and her boyfriend to take us to this place in a rented car. That would have been fine except that the friend did not know how to drive and had just taken lessons before our arrival! Oh well, we still had a wonderful time to look forward to, and we would trust the angels of God to take care of our transportation safety.

Off we went up a winding mountain road that had such bad pot holes in it that it would have blown a tire or broken something if we had hit one of them. He drove half of the time on the right side of the road and the other half of the time on the wrong side of the road, trying to avoid the horrible holes. At the same time, he was hoping not to meet another vehicle on a curve while driving in the wrong lane. I decided to close my eyes and relax despite the obvious dangers. Geri on the other hand was watching every move with heightened awareness.

Finally, by the grace of God, we arrived at our destination. It was a tiny village with dirt streets. The small, old hotel we were booked in had no air conditioning, and the temperature was very hot. That would not do at all for Geri who definitely needed cool air to sleep. We asked if there was any other hotel in the village. As would have been expected, the answer was NO! We then asked our escorting couple to please find any place that had beds and an air conditioner. After scouring the village, they found a man who did have a tiny (I said TINY) room with a window air conditioner where he would let us stay. Thank God!

It was now night, and no sooner had we gotten our suitcases in the room, when we got a call saying the bus was leaving for the beautiful pool of water under the stars. We certainly didn't want to miss that, so we grabbed our swim suits, and off we went.

The bus was a very old school bus with all the windows down on a hot night. As it rumbled up a dirt mountain road, the dust flew inside the bus. The locals didn't seem to notice this, as I'm sure they were used to it, but for two ladies from Dallas, it was a new experience. The road seemed to go on and on and on until finally, the driver stopped on a steep incline and told everyone to get out; we had arrived at our destination.

We were sure happy to finally get to the pool of water under the stars. We proceeded to hike farther up the mountain on foot—in the dark. Forget the stars or the moon. There was not the slightest glimmer of light on this night. Geri was afraid of snakes and refused to set foot on the mountain without a flashlight showing her every step in advance. Thankfully, the driver had a flashlight. He took her arm and led her, lighted step by lighted step, up the mountain.

Finally, we came to a fence and could go no further. Where was the beautiful pool of water? Nothing was there but rocks and bushes. What in the world were we doing here? We asked someone who spoke English and found out that this wasn't the pool at all. They had brought us as close to the top of a volcano as possible where we were supposed to be able to see the volcano apex. We could see nothing at all but blackness and, of course, the fence. We sat down on a rock for a few minutes and then trudged back down the mountain to the bus.

The trip continued down the mountain until the driver pulled off the side of the road and again told us to get out. Alas, we had finally arrived at the long awaited destination we had anticipated when we boarded our flight in Dallas—the beautiful pool of water—but this time on a starless night. We hiked down the mountainside where there was no road or even a trail. The pool was in the distance, but where were the changing rooms where we could put on our bathing suits? There were none! Everyone headed for the bushes to change clothes in the dark except Geri. The thought of snakes in the bushes was too much for her, so she went to the bank of the pool without changing clothes and sat down with her feet in the water.

When I arrived, I got in a pool of the running stream, which was heated by the volcano. I noticed Geri was squirming around, so I asked her what the problem was. She said that she was uncomfortable. As I waded toward the bank where she was sitting, I noticed that she had ants crawling all over her. I told her to get in the water immediately, clothes and all, so the ants would get off of her, which she did. She had sat down on top of an ant bed and had bites all over her legs and bottom. I asked her why she had not noticed them biting her. She said she was in such pain from the bumpy ride and the rocks she was sitting on that she thought that was the cause of her discomfort. We had no medication to ease the pain, so she just had to tolerate it the remainder of our three day "relaxing rest."

The next morning, we set the alarm for five a.m., got up, dressed, and went outside to stand by the street where a man was supposed to pick us up for a fishing trip. Of course, they said you have to get an early start to catch fish. There was a light drizzle as we stood in the dark.

After about fifteen minutes, a man drove up and said we could not fish that day because it was supposed to rain, but he would meet us the next morning at the same time and take us fishing. We certainly did not want to get up again at five a.m., but Geri had been looking forward to catching fish, especially the rainbow bass that were in the lake. That's right, rainbow <u>bass</u>. We knew about rainbow trout which we had caught in Colorado, but we never knew rainbow bass existed.

We were now starting the third and last day of our "rest," again waiting on the street in the dark at five-thirty a.m. The guide pulled up in a very, very old Range Rover pulling a little boat. He drove us to the lake, where he backed down a long, steep shoreline to the boat launch. This scared Geri half to death, but he said there was no other place to put the boat in the water, so she closed her eyes and prayed.

Geri with boat being launched for fishing trip in Costa Rica.

Once on the water, we all three began to fish. The guide caught several of the notorious rainbow bass, and after a while, I caught a couple of them also, but Geri caught none. Time was running out because we had to leave the village and head back to the city no later than noon to arrive in time for the opening night of the crusade. This whole fishing trip was just for Geri, and she was coming back empty-handed. Well at least we did get to see a real live rainbow bass with our own eyes.

By the time we packed the car and headed down the mountain toward the city with the boyfriend driving, a heavy fog had settled in. You could barely see your hand in front of your face, much less the pot holes in the road. There wasn't much oncoming traffic on that country road, but you couldn't see that very well either. It was nerve racking to watch this inexperienced driver try to maneuver in these terrible driving conditions.

After driving about an hour down the mountain, an oncoming car stopped us to say that the bridge ahead had been washed out and the road was impassable. We now had to turn around and drive all the way back up the mountain to the village we had come from and find a longer alternative route to the city. By this time, Geri had "had it" and asked me to take over the driving, so I did. To say driving in these conditions was difficult is an understatement. Every moment you had to be on high alert because of the dense fog and mammoth pot holes.

By the time we drove back up the mountain and down it another way, we were exhausted and very late getting back to the city. In fact, the crusade meeting had already been going on for an hour when we arrived at our motel. I debated as to whether I should even go or not because it was so very late. But I decided I had to go, no matter what the time was—since I was the speaker for this crusade.

I quickly changed clothes and drove to the crusade. I had learned many years ago from my pastor that in ministry, you must be like an Eveready flashlight battery—ready in season and out of season. The Holy Spirit just needs us to show up and yield to Him, trusting that He will accomplish the perfect will of the Father. After all it is "not by might, nor by power, but by my Spirit, saith the Lord of hosts" (Zech. 4:6). He took over my weary body, and the meeting was a success. **All Jesus needs is a body.**

One night while holding an open-air meeting for the city, I wanted to teach about the blood of Jesus. There was much demonic activity there, and I felt strongly that the people needed to understand the power of the blood of our Lord. I wanted a visible way to demonstrate to them that they could plead the blood of Jesus over their homes, their children or anything else and that His blood would create a protective barrier. I wanted them to have some anointing oil also. So I went to a local store and bought many small bottles. I filled them with cooking oil and put a few drops of red food coloring in each bottle to symbolize the blood of Jesus. The thing I didn't think about in advance was that the water-based food coloring would not mix with the oil, so each drop of red was floating by itself in a sea of oil. If you shook the bottle the two substances would still not mix, the red droplets simply became smaller and more numerous.

It was too late to prepare some different bottles, for the meeting was to start shortly. So I took all the bottles of oil and "blood," and after explaining what they meant and how to use them, I passed them out to everyone at the end of the meeting. I often wondered afterwards what happened to the walls of their homes when they smeared that red food coloring on them.

Anyway, God knew what that symbolized, and I am sure He honored it. If it did leave their walls with permanent red streaks, they would have a continual reminder of the blood of Jesus, which would be a good thing.

During that week of meetings, many people gave their lives to Christ. After explaining the meaning of water baptism, they wanted to follow Jesus in that experience. We moved the last service indoors, into the sponsoring church and set up an "induction center," to induct people into the army of God. What a glorious night, as many were baptized and many more made a commitment to follow Jesus as part of His worldwide army. The angels rejoiced greatly, and so did we!

Radical Seeds

When I was a young, Spirit-filled Christian, I joined a small but growing church, which I loved. I had not been a member very long, when one Sunday morning, the pastor said God had told him to challenge the people to give a tithe on what they <u>wanted</u> to receive. I had never heard of such a thing. What a fabulous opportunity this was from God. If you wanted your annual income to be fifty thousand dollars, you would give an offering of five thousand. If you wanted your annual income to be one hundred thousand dollars, you would give an offering of ten thousand dollars, etc. In my mind, this was a promise from God and an opportunity that was too good to pass up.

So I emptied all of my bank accounts and gave that money to the Lord, believing with all my heart that what I gave would be a tithe on what He would give me back. That was sowing **radical seeds**. I couldn't understand why everyone in the church didn't do the same. In fact, the pastor asked me to speak to the congregation that night and encourage them to take advantage of this great challenge from God.

I stood very strong in faith, <u>expecting</u> God to do what the pastor had explained to us, and He did not disappoint me. It took two years for that to become a reality in my finances. That catapulted me into a greater ability to give than I had ever had before. The Lord continued to challenge me over all the years to give greatly. And as I obeyed Him and gave **radical seeds,** He always saw to it that it was given back to me, "good measure, pressed down, shaken together, and running over" (Luke 6:38).

At the time I emptied my bank accounts and gave the funds to Jesus, I had not heard about seed time and harvest in the realm of finances, but I was operating in it anyway. I later came to understand that there are two different types of giving.

First there is the tithe, which is the <u>first</u> ten percent of the money you have already received. This is what we <u>owe</u> God. According to Malachi 3:8-9, we are robbing God if we do not give Him the first ten percent. "Will a man rob God? Yet ye have robbed me. But ye say, Wherein have we robbed thee? In <u>tithes</u> and <u>offerings</u>. Ye are cursed with a curse: for ye have robbed me...."

People wonder why they are having so much financial stress or other problems in their lives. Well, try robbing God, and see how far you get! If you obey Him by giving tithes and offerings, He says He will rebuke the devourer for you, which is definitely what we want. If you do not tithe and give offerings, then the devourer has freedom to steal whatever he wants from your life.

You don't have to be very smart to figure out that it is best to obey God and give Him what belongs to Him, which is the <u>first</u> ten percent of your income, plus offerings. You can't pay all of your bills before giving tithes to God, and then hope to have a little left over to give Him. That is backwards and will not work. The likelihood is that you will <u>never</u> have ten percent left over. You will probably not have enough to cover your bills because you did not honor God with your tithe.

The second kind of giving is not a certain percent like tithing; it is a free will offering, given to God as seed for a <u>future</u> harvest. I want you to see the difference clearly. The tithe is ten percent of money you have <u>already received</u>, but offerings are seeds for a financial harvest you <u>want to receive in the future</u>. That is what you give Him out of your heart.

Let's look at the seeds this way: If you were a farmer, and you had 10 bags of seed, you could decide how many bags you would set aside to keep and how many bags you would plant as seed for your future harvest. If you decide to keep 9 bags and plant 1 bag of seeds, you would get a small harvest. If you decided to keep 3 bags and plant 7 bags of seeds, you would get a much, much larger harvest. It would be up to you to decide how much you wanted to keep and how much you wanted to plant, and your harvest would be commensurate with the seed you planted.

That is such a simple and clear illustration of how we should view our finances. You might be thinking, "How can I plant seed when it takes all 10 bags to pay my bills and feed my family?"

Let me assure you that God's word works. He is not a man that He should lie. If you will step out in faith on God's word and give Him the first ten percent, plus offerings, you will be amazed at how well the remainder will cover your needs.

Let's look at an example: Let's assume that planting 1 bag of seed yields 10 bags of harvested seed. Let's also assume that the farmer has 10 bags to start with.

If he keeps 10 bags and plants 0 bags of seed, he gets **0** harvest. (This guy would be living on "Barely Get Along Street.")

If he keeps 9 bags and plants <u>1 bag</u>, he will get <u>**10 bags**</u> harvested.

If he decides to keep 8 bags and plant <u>2 bags</u> the next year, then he will harvest twice as much. That's <u>**20 bags**</u>.

The next year he has much more available to plant and to keep, so he decides to keep 10 bags and plant <u>10 bags</u>, which yields **100 bags** of harvest.

Now he has 100 bags. So if he decides to keep 15 bags and sow <u>85 bags</u>, he will receive **850 bags** of harvest.

In this example, it is logical and easy to see how his harvest increased as he planted more seed each year. That is what happens to farmers in the natural. That is also what happens to seeds of finances that are planted in the good soil of the kingdom of God.

Let's say the last example is you, and you have received 850 bags of money for last year's labor. First of all, the tithe belongs to God. So the first 85 bags of money should be given to Him. You now have 765 bags of money to live on and do with as you please.

Let's assume these 765 bags of money represent wealth above your needs. (Sounds good, doesn't it?) You could give 65 bags as a free will offering to God and buy a new house with the remaining 700 bags if you wanted to. Or you could keep 65 bags for yourself and give 700 bags to God as a freewill offering, which would make you a paymaster in God's kingdom.

If this money was sown into a place that was vigorously saving souls, then you would be instrumental in bringing many people into heaven that could otherwise go to hell. That sounds very graphic, but it is the truth. "You shall know the truth and the truth shall make you free" (John 8:32).

Some people are sent out to evangelize, and others are called to pay their way. Both are partners in saving souls, and both will receive rewards from God. If you really see this, and you really care about people's eternal destiny, then you will want to put as much money as possible into the kingdom of God. But be wise, and put it into ground where <u>eternal</u> fruit grows.

God has a way of doing things that confounds the human understanding. If you are in deep debt and you want to recover from it, the best thing to do is give to God. It seems counterintuitive to gain by giving, but that is God's recovery plan.

"One man gives freely, yet gains even more; another withholds unduly, but comes to poverty" (Prov. 11:24 NIV).

A righteous man walks by <u>faith</u> and not by sight. It works! I know because I have tried it.

I am always happy when God tells me to plant **radical seeds** because I have learned that He is trying to make a way to bless me in bigger and better ways. If you respond to His challenge to give, it opens the door for Him to bless you in a greater way, which is what is in His heart to do. If a person is stingy and disobedient, he has shut the door to God's blessings. Any good parent would not reward their child for being disobedient, and God would not either. Obedience is better than sacrifice. If you don't <u>tithe</u> and <u>give</u> offerings as God commands, then you <u>will</u> sacrifice, whether you like it or not!

What you sow is what you will reap. "He which sows sparingly shall reap also sparingly; and he which sows bountifully shall reap also bountifully. Every man according as he purposes in his heart, so let him give; not grudgingly, or of necessity: for God loves a cheerful giver" (2 Cor. 9:6-7). Some want to sow sparingly and then reap bountifully. It does not work like that—not for the farmer, and not for you. So be extravagant in your giving to God, and sow **radical seeds.**

The Surgical "Mistake"

In 1995, I had just brought my Chinese nurse, Doreen, to America to train her as my assistant in eye surgery. About the same time, I had gone to the American Academy of Ophthalmology meeting, where reports of new techniques and discoveries in medicine are always discussed.

One of the doctors that year reported his discovery that cataract removal could be done under topical anesthesia. That means you could do the surgery by deadening the eye with anesthetic eye drops only, instead of using an injection around the eye to deaden it as we had been doing for decades.

I thought this was very radical, and I was not interested in doing this on my patients.

One morning not long after this, I had seven cataract removals scheduled. Doreen was my "scrub nurse," which means she would be the one handing me instruments, sutures, medicines or anything else I might need during surgery. The "circulating nurse" was a man from a temporary nursing service that had never helped me before. In fact, I had never seen him before that day nor did I ever see him after that day. He would be handing the things to Doreen that we needed during the cases.

While I was in the middle of my last case, the nurse who was the head of all surgery in that hospital came to me and whispered in my ear that she needed to see me after I finished my last case. She had never made a request like that before, and I wondered what she could want. All of the surgeries went very well. When I finished, I went to see what she had to tell me.

I was shocked when she said that before my surgery began, she had personally prepared seven syringes of the anesthetic solution that we used to deaden the eye by injecting it around the eye. She said that six of them had been used, and there was still one syringe left. That meant that one of the seven cases I had just finished had been done with topical anesthesia only. I had no idea which patient had not gotten the injection of anesthesia because I had used a syringe full on each patient. One of the syringes must have had saline in it instead of anesthetic.

Here was a shocking new revelation to me. If I as the surgeon could not tell the difference, and the patient could not tell the difference, then why use injections of anesthetic any more. From that day forward, I never injected anesthesia on another case of cataract removal. I used topical anesthesia exclusively.

That made quite a difference to the patient, because they could see immediately after surgery with topical anesthesia, and a bandage was not necessary. On the other hand, the injected anesthetic would blur vision after surgery, and a bandage was necessary. With it, there was always the possibility of bleeding from the injection, as well as more swelling from the extra fluid around the eye.

This discovery helped me with surgery in China also, because I needed fewer supplies, and the patients recovered faster. Doreen had a brother with cataracts, and she asked me if I would do his surgery on my next trip to China. I was happy to do that. On the day of his surgery, I did a routine cataract extraction using only topical anesthesia. I later found out that the Chinese ophthalmologists had been curious about the surgery, so they took her brother straight from surgery down to the eye clinic to examine his eye and check his vision. He saw 20/20 out of the operated eye immediately after surgery. Needless to say, they were impressed.

I tell you this story because I feel sure this "mistake" was really the hand of God nudging me to do surgery that would be better for my patients in America and in China or wherever He sends me. He knew I would definitely be resistant to doing surgery with topical anesthesia only, so He showed me how beneficial it was through this "mistake."

I never knew whether it was Doreen or the temporary circulating nurse that neglected to give me the injection of anesthesia on one case. That doesn't really matter because it was ordained by God to help me and the countless people I have operated on after that day. I am very grateful to Him for leading and guiding me. Sometimes He has to be a little sneaky to get me to do it, but His will always prevails in my life. Thank God!

Chapter 12

Miracles

The Tambourine Miracle

We were scheduled to preach in a number of different places in Costa Rica on a mission trip. A rural church where we ministered had an orphanage they had built, so many children were in that service.

One small child was sitting close to me, so I could easily watch her as she praised God the best she knew how. Next to her there was an older girl who had a tambourine. From time to time, the older girl would set the tambourine down, and the little girl would try to pick it up. Each time she tried, the older girl would immediately pick the tambourine back up and start playing it again. I felt so sorry for this tiny one who was about four or five years old.

She was wearing a dress that was several sizes too large for her, obviously a hand-me-down from an older child. The hem came almost to the floor. She wore little "jelly shoes." Above all, she really wanted to play a tambourine but was never given the opportunity. As the praise and worship continued, the broken down tambourine played by the older girl began to come apart, and two of the metal jingles fell off onto the floor. The little girl got down on the floor and crawled under some chairs to retrieve the two jingles. She placed one of them in her right hand and one in her left hand and began trying to clap them together like mini cymbals. She seemed so happy to at least have something to praise God with, even though it was extremely meager. Don't you know the joy this gave the Lord to see someone praising Him with all their might from their heart?

The next day, we looked in every shop we could find in San Jose, trying to find a tambourine for that little girl. We wanted her to have one of her very own. We knew that would thrill her and could possibly be the best gift she had ever received in her life. Despite our best efforts, we found no shop that carried tambourines. We were very disappointed by this, but had to leave the city for our next preaching assignment in another town.

On the way, our driver stopped to get gas at a small station near a banana plantation, which was many miles away from anything. As we got out of the car to stretch our legs, there was a station wagon parked next to our car, and the back seat was full of…you guessed it, tambourines. What in the world was anyone doing on this country road with a car full of tambourines? Obviously, the man had to be a tambourine salesman. Only God can cause a "coincidence" like that! The one thing we had been searching for all over a big city was now parked next to us on a two lane country road—and not just one of them, but a whole car load!

The Bible says, God does exceeding abundantly above all you can ask or think. Well, He just did it! We immediately found the owner of the station wagon and asked if we could buy a tambourine. Of course he was delighted to make a sale, and we were delighted to have found a tambourine at last.

We sent it back to the little child at the orphanage, who I know played it with great vigor and joy. I'm sure it made her smile. It certainly made us smile, and I believe it made God smile to know that His miracle made us all so happy.

The Manger Miracle

In 2006, I had been practicing medicine for many years, and in my heart, I was ready to sell my practice and retire. I still loved the surgery and the patient care, but the administrative aspects of the practice were taxing and tiring.

It was at this time that the building where I had my office was sold, and we were told that high-rise apartments would be built in its place. This put me in a position of looking for a new office space and going to the considerable expense of completely rebuilding the interior to create examining rooms to meet my needs. Instead of retiring, I now faced the huge project of finding a suitable new location, moving all my medical charts and expensive examination equipment there, and notifying all of my patients of my new location. This prospect did not thrill me to say the least.

As I began the tedious project of looking for new office space with a commercial real estate broker, my friend Geri told me that the Lord had shown her that my new office would be like a manger. God would draw people there by His Spirit to come to Jesus, just like He brought the three wise men to the manger in Bethlehem. Of course, this word from God excited me, and my attitude toward building a new office changed immediately. I was now looking forward with great anticipation to what God was going to do.

As the search continued, the broker took me to many buildings. None of them seemed right, until we came to one building that housed professional people like attorneys, accountants, architects, etc., but no doctors. The only acceptable space that was available was on the seventh floor in a corner of the building. I felt like that was the location God had chosen for

His manger, so I signed a lease. As I was looking at the layout of the space and trying to fit my examination rooms, waiting room, and offices for my employees into it, the only logical positioning of my private office was in the very corner of this corner space.

I drew the new floor plan, and the contractor went to work, knocking down walls and building new ones in different locations. It was really a big mess for a while, but then it began taking shape, and our excitement grew. Finally, the day came when the last walls were painted and the front door was put in place.

By the front desk, I had hung a huge picture of Jesus smiling as He held a little sparrow on His finger. I chose a glass front door so that people could see this picture as they walked down the hall from the elevators to my office. I also had an intercom system installed so I could play soft Christian instrumental music in the background as patients waited to be seen. Every room had a copy of my book, *An Instrument in God's Hand*, in it for inspirational reading and a small booklet explaining salvation. The office was decorated with pictures and furnishings to bring honor to the King of Kings.

The day came for the movers to move all of our things from the old office to the new office. I had emptied my big, executive desk at my old office before the move, and they placed it in my new private office facing the windows. The exterior walls of the building were entirely glass, so there was a spectacular view of Dallas from my private office in the corner, which had glass walls to the north as well as to the west. In all my years of practicing medicine, I had never had such a gorgeous office.

I started dusting out the drawers to my desk before putting things back in them. In the very back of one drawer, there was a post card that I had not seen when I emptied the drawer before the move. I was totally amazed as I pulled it out and saw a picture of the **manger** in Bethlehem on the card. I looked at the back of the card and saw that it had been mailed to me from Israel eighteen years before by a friend, and apparently lost in the recesses of that drawer to be found on this very day—the day the manger was born. How great is our God, and how full of wonderful surprises. This card was of course a strong confirmation of what God had told Geri about my office being a manger.

Two days later, on February 2, 2007, I went to my hairdresser to have my hair cut, and he had a Christmas card with a **manger** scene on his window ledge. This was puzzling since it was now five weeks past Christmas, and that was the only card he had kept. I asked why he had it there, at which point he picked it up and handed it to me saying, "Here, you take it." This was the second confirmation of God's word to me about the manger.

On February 20, 2007, I received a gift from a Chinese doctor from Kunming, China. This was a doctor I had met briefly many years ago in Beijing, when I was teaching modern cataract surgery there. It was a shock to be receiving a gift from someone that I barely knew and an even greater shock when I opened the gift. It was a woven tapestry of…you guessed it—a **manger**. Baby Jesus and mother Mary had Chinese facial features. Even the animals looked Chinese. This was a third miraculous confirmation and a precious gift to be treasured.

God performed exactly what He said He would do. The office had a wonderful atmosphere of peace that people loved. In fact, employees from other offices in the building would come there just to relax in the peace of God they felt there. People were drawn to the Savior as they listened to the music, looked at the pictures, and read the available literature. God had surely made my office **His manger** and confirmed it through amazing miracles.

The Airline Miracle

We were scheduled for a series of flights on a mission trip, starting from Dallas to Tokyo nonstop, then to Beijing, where I would be teaching eye surgeons modern techniques of cataract removal. After teaching and demonstrating the surgery in China, we were to fly to Singapore for a short visit and then on to Jakarta, Indonesia, where we had about a week of preaching engagements scheduled in various churches. After sharing God's word and power in Indonesia, we were to fly to Tokyo and then back to Dallas.

When the day of departure came, Geri dropped me off at the airline terminal to check in while she parked the car. I handed the tickets to the airline agent who laid them on her desk and began typing things into her computer. She continued to type on and on, for a long time without saying a word to me. We had travelled a great deal, and I was puzzled by her activity. After a long wait, I finally asked her what was going on. She replied that the tickets for the entire trip had not been confirmed properly by the travel agent, and therefore, they had all been cancelled! She was trying to reschedule some semblance of what we had lost.

I was stunned. All those people abroad were counting on us to be there on our scheduled days, and now the entire trip was in jeopardy. I stood there patiently and began to pray fervently. I was praying not only that the tickets would be restored to the original itinerary, but also that it would be accomplished before Geri returned because I knew their loss would "send her into orbit." As Geri walked into the terminal from parking the car, the ticket agent handed me our new tickets and said that she had been able to reschedule us on the exact same flights. How very difficult it is to reschedule even one flight at the last minute much less this entire itinerary. God had done another miracle in front of my eyes!

The only difference was that she could not get us our same good seats and had to put us in the only seats available on all the flights. The first and longest segment of our journey, from Dallas to Tokyo, was going to take about 13 hours, and the only seats left on that crowded flight were in the middle of the center section. That was bad news for me, because I had planned to prepare all my lectures for the doctors in Beijing during that flight, and the seat assignment I now had was going to be like a squeezed shut accordion with no room to work.

I asked the ticket agent if there was any way possible to get a different seat, and she said that every single seat had been sold out for that flight and the only chance would be if someone failed to show up. She suggested that we ask the agent at the gate for help, so we did. That agent told us to stand by the loading ramp until everyone had been loaded.

As we watched people go by, I had the bright idea to ask about the possibility of an upgrade to business class. I walked back to the agent at the desk who told me that the upgrade would cost several thousand dollars and that no seats were available anyway. Forget that bright idea! When every last soul had entered the plane, the only two empty seats left were our two in the center section. So we took our seats, thankful to at least be on the plane. I opened all my books and papers and began studying while the plane was still on the ground.

In a few minutes, a flight attendant came over and knelt by Geri's seat. He leaned over and said softly to me, "Aren't you Dr. Vaughan?" I told him I was. He said, "You did surgery on my eyes a few years ago, and I have seen very well since then. I saw you asking the gate agent for an upgrade to business class, but there were no seats available. Would you like to move up to first class at no charge?"

How fast do you think a little lady in an accordion seat can move? I grabbed my things and was out of there like greased lightning, and Geri was not far behind! He seated me in the far right seat in the first row of first class in that huge 747 and seated Geri in the far left seat of the first row of first class.

I have no idea what Geri did, but I immediately opened my books and papers again and now began studying on my large tray with plenty of "elbow space." I worked diligently for those thirteen hours with the exception of a short break for a dinner of filet mignon with the trimmings, a hot fudge sundae made with Haagen-Dazs ice cream, and a box of Godiva chocolates to enjoy later.

One could get used to this very easily! The grace (unmerited favor) of God and His profound love toward His children was shown forth once again by doing the impossible. What a miracle He had done for us!

Afterword

Thank you for allowing me to share some of my life's adventures with you through this book. None of what I have shared would have been possible if I had not taken a first step on this journey many years ago. That first step was to give my life to Jesus and tell Him He could use it anyway He chose. I had no idea what He would do with me, but this book reflects some of the adventures He has led me on.

My deepest desire is that you too will give your life to Jesus. We cannot really conceive of the enormous love God has for us. He is waiting with open arms to receive you and begin to use YOU as His hands and His mouthpiece. God has already done all He can do for us by giving His Son, Jesus Christ, to die for us. So the next step is up to us. I have included the following scriptures for you to consider.

I pray with all my heart that you step into Jesus' arms and decide to follow Him forever. Take the first step and pray this simple prayer from your heart today, for we never know which day might be our last one on this earth.

Scriptures:

"For God so loved the world, that he gave his only begotten Son, that whosoever believeth in (trusts, clings to, relies on) Him should not perish, but have everlasting life." –John 3:16

"If you shall confess with thy mouth the Lord Jesus, and shall believe in your heart that God hath raised him from the dead, you shall be saved. For with the heart man believeth unto righteousness; and with the mouth confession is made unto salvation." –Romans 10:9-10

"For whosoever shall call upon the name of the Lord shall be saved." –Romans 10:13

Prayer of Salvation

Dear Father,

I ask you to forgive me of my sins. Wash me clean in the blood of Jesus, and set me free from all hindrances. Give me a brand new start in life. I believe that Jesus Christ is the Son of God, that He died for me, and rose from the dead. I confess that Jesus is my Lord and my Savior. I give my life to You and ask You to use it anyway You want. Fill me with the Holy Spirit, and make me a powerful witness for You.

Thank You for hearing my prayer, for forgiving me, for loving me, and for preparing a home for me in heaven, in Jesus' name. Amen.

About the Author

Dr. Elizabeth R. Vaughan received her BA degree at the University of Texas, where she was chosen "Outstanding Student." She graduated from Southwestern Medical School and did her residency in ophthalmology at Parkland Memorial Hospital in Dallas, Texas. She did postgraduate training at Harvard Medical School.

Her honors include: World's Who's Who of Women (1979-80), Who's Who in Texas (1973-74), Who's Who of American Women (1974-75), and International Who's Who of Intellectuals (1980). She held memberships in the American Medical Association, the Texas Medical Association, the Dallas County Medical Association, the Christian Medical Society, the American Academy of Ophthalmology, the American Society of Cataract and Refractive Surgery, and the International Society of Refractive Surgery. She was on the clinical faculty of Southwestern Medical School in Dallas, teaching eye surgery.

Since her commitment to the Lord Jesus, she has traveled throughout the world, sharing the love of Jesus and His healing power. She has ministered in many unusual places, including Russia, Costa Rica, Israel, Jamaica, China, Indonesia, Mexico and South Africa. She has been a guest on many television programs, including CBN, TBN, PTL, That's Incredible, and The Phil Donohue Show. She also built a 5-million watt television station in the Dallas Metroplex. She was hostess of a live daily Christian TV show and was heard on radio for many years.

Dr. Vaughan had a large practice of ophthalmology in Dallas, where patients came from as far away as Pakistan and South America to have her do their eye surgery. She opened an eye surgery center in Beijing, where surgery was done free of charge for poor, blind people. The first mobile examination unit was launched in June 1999 to reach those in need that live in remote areas of China, such as Inner Mongolia.

Contact information:

Elizabeth Vaughan Ministries, Inc.

P.O. Box 454

Argyle, TX 76226

Website: www.godsinstrument.com

Recommended Reading

An Instrument in God's Hand, by Elizabeth R. Vaughan, M.D.

I Play the Notes, but He Makes the Music, by Geri Hudson Morgan